C000233265

Edmund Burke and Our Present Discontents

Edmund Burke and Our Present Discontents

Jim McCue

The Claridge Press

1997

First published in Great Britain 1997

by The Claridge Press
33 Canonbury Park South
London N1 2JW

All rights reserved. No part of this publication may be reproduced, stored in a retrieval system or transmitted in any form or by any means without the prior written permission of the publisher, nor be otherwise circulated in any form of binding or cover other than that in which it is published.

© Jim McCue 1997

CIP data for this title is available from the British Library

ISBN 1 870626 17 6

Printed and bound by Antony Rowe Ltd,
Bumpers Farm, Chippenham, Wiltshire

Contents

Preface

Edmund Burke died two hundred years ago, but many of the problems he addressed have since intensified, and although his insights are neglected they remain supremely pertinent. Coleridge gave his warrant for a study such as this when he wrote "I cannot conceive of a time or a state of things in which the writings of Edmund Burke will not have the highest value." In bringing Burke's work to bear upon modern discontents, this book includes a good number of recent cases and commentaries to illustrate a larger argument about society. The focus throughout is on Britain, but with proper regard to circumstances some of the ideas might be extrapolated to much of the West.

Every book about Burke is liable to become an anthology, because his writing is manly, precise and irresistibly quotable. His expression can rarely be bettered. This is not, however, a work of scholarship, so spellings and punctuation have been modernized. Unfortunately, no edition of Burke is standard, and the ongoing Oxford edition of *The Writings and Speeches* is unsatisfactory in some respects. Writers on Burke cite from a wide range of incompatible and inaccessible editions, so it has seemed to me best simply to give the titles of works substantially quoted.

I am most grateful to David Blundell, Sue Corbett, Ian Crowe, Pat Fenteman, Richard Luckett, Tim Moore, Conor Cruise O'Brien, Peter Riddell and Laurie Weston for information, help and their friendship.

I am also grateful to Valerie Eliot and to Faber & Faber for permission to quote from *Collected Poems 1909–1962* by T. S. Eliot.

I

The Same Mistakes

> Men have been sometimes led by degrees, sometimes hurried into things, of which, if they could have seen the whole together, they never would have permitted the most remote approach.
>
> (*Reflections*.)

As we look back over the most destructive century in history, and uneasily forward to a millennium likely to be violently disordered and morally bewildering, we may well wonder where we went wrong. Edmund Burke offers some answers. He was the first person to warn that the modern world was losing its way. He passionately attacked the kinds of fundamentalism that had begun to emerge at the end of the 18th century and that have dogged us ever since. He argued that the French revolutionaries were mad to remove so many of the props of civil society on a theory, and predicted, though he did not live to see, the whole tragic course of their experiment.

Since then, theory after theory has been tried, and the tragedy has been played out in many guises. Yet much Western thinking is still under the spell of the same "cannibal philosophy". So Burke's analysis is as valid now as it was two centuries ago, and his ideas relate remarkably well to our present discontents. He has much to say about representative government; about the shortcomings of materialism; about the importance of property-owning and heredity; about class; about families and relations between the sexes; about why a written constitution can never live up to its promises; about the invasion of the state into private life; about the limits of government; and about tolerance and pluralism. As the original Eurosceptic he wrote at length about Britain's relations with an expansionist European superstate. But most of all, he had a profound knowledge of the complexities of human nature.

At a time when the United Kingdom may be facing constitutional disintegration into separate parts, we can learn from his magnanimous insistence, when George III faced the loss of the

American colonies, that everyone benefits when interests are reconciled, rather than set at odds. And at a time of moral disintegration – when crime is rampant and civic responsibility, restraint and decency are in retreat before individualism, greed and vulgarity – his analysis of France's descent into chaos is a grim warning.

Burke thought the French revolutionaries were sophistical barbarians; now a Labour MP speaks of "the new barbarianism". The signs of a society breaking down, a society in which large numbers of people do not feel bound by any rules or loyalties, are unmistakable. In the media, in advertising, public relations, the welfare state and even the Royal Family, decadence is so commonplace that we think it normal, until now and again we step back and see that this behaviour and these priorities are unsustainable, destructive, delusive – crazed. How would it be if everyone behaved so cynically? Burke thought that his society was going mad and countenancing its own destruction; much of ours appears bent on doing the same.

What he deplored about the French Revolution was the overturning of an established order and morality by a flattery of the masses which pretended that their unguided opinions and appetites could be relied upon to produce a virtuous and equitable society. He described his fears and his reaction in a letter of January 31, 1792:

> When I saw all this mingled scene of crime, of vice, of disorder, of folly, and of madness, received by very many here, not with the horror and disgust which it ought to have produced, but with rapture and exultation, as some almost supernatural benefit showered down upon the race of mankind; and when I saw that arrangements were publicly made for communicating to these Islands their full share of these blessings, I thought myself bound to stand out and by every means in my power to distinguish the ideas of a sober and virtuous liberty (such as I thought our party had ever cultivated) from that profligate, immoral, impious, and rebellious licence, which, through the medium of every sort of disorder and calamity, conducts to some kind or other of tyrannic domination.

The ideas of the French Revolution, under their simplistic banners – "liberty, equality, fraternity" – have left, as Burke said in the same letter, "an example in Europe never to be effaced", and many of today's follies can be traced back to that example. In this new age of false feeling and indecorum, Burke's strictures find many applications. How, then, can we learn from him?

First, we should discard the myth of the reactionary apologist for an outdated form of rule. Burke is now more travestied than read. Little of his work is available in popular editions, and even on university courses in politics or history he is rarely a compulsory component. In *Citizens*, his 875-page chronicle of the French Revolution, Simon Schama finds no space for Burke's views or for his influence on events. It is thought safe to ignore Burke when considering his own age, let alone ours. He is supposed the final advocate of a corrupt and repressive *ancien régime* which could not last. He is depicted as complacently arguing for injustice. He is believed to have favoured the *status quo*, or even the *status quo ante*, irrespective of what it might be. It is argued that he was opposed to all progress, which washed over him and made him irrelevant; that history didn't take any notice of him, and that therefore he must have been wrong. A. J. P. Taylor went further, dismissing him as "a corrupt Whig hack". So it may come as a surprise that Burke's political credo was highly principled and that he was personally responsible for extensive reforms. Burke was a lifelong liberal who knew that liberty without discipline meant only anarchy. Perhaps the modern depreciations of him are a reaction against the veneration of the 19th century, when De Quincey described him as "the supreme writer of his century, the man of largest and finest understanding" and Macaulay called him "the greatest man since Milton".

But injustice to Burke's memory is a matter mainly for historians. More important is what he can tell us about ourselves. For although – or else because – his political reflections were always written in response to immediate circumstances, and never as a codified philosophy, they have an extraordinary valency. His political thought is perhaps the most sustained and sophisticated of any age, and against it we can measure the extremity and dogmatism of our own politics. Judged by his values, most people in public life today are fundamentalists, fanatical in their attachment to individual freedom of choice, whatever the social cost, and in their obeisance to majorities. Burke can show us how to rethink – with a recaptured subtlety and moderation – our ideas about rights, about democracy and consent, about equality and equity, and about how to achieve political accommodations that do not spawn mistrust and discontent.

Speaking on Fox's East India Bill in 1783, Burke commended the wisdom of his Irish compatriot: "Dr Swift somewhere says, that he who could make two blades of grass grow where but one grew before, was a greater benefactor to the human race than all the politicians that ever existed." Burke's own effort was not dissimilar. He believed, for instance, that the benefits of free trade could multiply wealth in this way. "Trade is not a limited thing, as if the objects of mutual demand and consumption could not stretch beyond the bounds of our jealousies," he wrote in 1778 to a firm of Bristol iron merchants who wanted him to take a protectionist stance. "It is hard to persuade us that everything which is *got* by another is not *taken* from ourselves. But it is fit that we should get the better of these suggestions. . ."

Personally, he was admirably resistant to such jealousies. Like Menenius Agrippa, the friend of Coriolanus, he saw that the organs of the body would harm themselves by conspiring against one another. Accordingly, Burke acted not narrowly on behalf of himself or of particular interests, but on behalf of the whole body of men. He wanted to promote the general welfare and to render "every act of power at the same time an act of lenity – the result of English bounty". Like an economist who avoids contentions about the exactly just division of resources, preferring to find ways to increase them, he wanted not to haggle over the distribution of authority – who decides what – but to make the decisions wise and equitable. He aimed to extend both the basis and the benefits of good government. His opponents, he wrote, "are always considering the formal distributions of power in a constitution: the moral basis they consider as nothing. Very different is my opinion: I consider the moral basis as everything."

Burke understood the tide of events better than any man, but his message has been obscured, over the past two hundred years, by the very jealousies and confusions, the failures and genocidal disasters that he uniquely foresaw. Belatedly, as we learn more about those, we are starting to appreciate his stature. He is to politics what his friend Adam Smith is to economics: the bedrock of a true understanding of the subject. And as more and more of his predictions are seen to have been realized, so interest is increasing in Burkean prescriptions.

2

An Extraordinary Man

Edmund Burke was born in Ireland in January 1729, the second son of a Dublin lawyer. His father, Richard, had married Mary Nagle in 1724, and they had 14 or 15 children, all of whom died young except Garrett, Edmund, Richard and Julia.

The children's mother was a Roman Catholic from Co. Cork. Their father had almost certainly converted recently from Catholicism to the Established Church, and all his life Edmund was reticent about this aspect of his background, and vulnerable to attack over it. Although he was brought up ostensibly as a Protestant, many of those he loved were Catholic, and this instilled in him a lifelong tolerance of religious difference. "I am attached", he wrote in his maturity, "to Christianity at large."

At six, he was sent to live with his maternal uncle, Patrick Nagle, in Ballyduff in Co. Cork, where he apparently attended a "hedge school", an illegal Catholic school giving instruction in the open air. In 1741, aged 12, he moved much closer to Dublin and its conformities: to a school at Ballitore, Co. Kildare, run by a Quaker, Abraham Shackleton, for whom Burke learnt the greatest respect. Here he became friends with the schoolmaster's son, Richard Shackleton, who later reported that Burke had been "particularly delighted with history and poetry" and had made the classics "his diversion rather than his business".

From Ballitore, Burke moved in 1744 to Trinity College, Dublin, where Oliver Goldsmith was among his contemporaries. Burke's studies were sufficiently distinguished for him to become a Scholar of the House as soon as he was eligible, in 1746, but his pursuits were not narrowly academic: he also took part in a literary or debating club, and founded and largely wrote a weekly paper, *The Reformer*, which ran for 13 issues.

After graduating from Trinity in 1748, he was destined for a career in the law. He enrolled at Middle Temple in London in May 1750, but his legal studies were desultory and he was never called to the Bar. In 1755, his father, finding that Edmund was devoting himself to literature, entertainment, travel and debating, cut his allowance, leaving him to make his own way. With wide interests but no fortune, Burke evidently toiled industriously. On the ladder to political eminence, he climbed on every rung. "I was not," he wrote at the end of his life, ". . . swaddled, and rocked, and dandled into a legislator. . . At every step of my progress in life (for in every step was I traversed and opposed), and at every turn-pike I met, I was obliged to show my passport".

The first result of his labours was a satirical essay, *A Vindication of Natural Society*, which appeared in 1756. This took a stage further the atheistic rationalism of the late Henry St John, Viscount Bolingbroke, demonstrating ironically that reason might overthrow not only revealed religion, but all social and civil institutions. The argument Burke mounts is so deceptively plausible, and its flaws are so well disguised, that the book was taken by several critics, including Warburton and Chesterfield, to be a genuine work of Bolingbroke's. To have his *reductio ad absurdum* taken at face value was a tribute to Burke's virtuosity, but he must have been shaken by the implications of such mistakings and alarmed by the momentum already gathering behind ideas he abhorred. In the second edition, he explained that his design had been to show how easy it was "to maintain a wrong cause, and to support paradoxical opinions to the satisfaction of a common auditory", so illustrating the destructive danger of sceptical sophistry. Indirectly, his final works, on the French Revolution, are an attack on the very position he had pretended to take up more than 30 years before.

Shortly afterwards, Burke published *A Philosophical Enquiry into the Origin of Our Ideas of the Sublime and Beautiful*, his only book of pure philosophy. Despite being a specialized account of aesthetics, it was a prompt and lasting success, running into 15 editions in the author's lifetime.

These two books were published by the Dodsley brothers, who from 1759 onwards paid Burke £100 a year to produce *The Annual Register*. Editing this influential miscellany until 1788, and for many years writing the bulk of it himself (including its "Historical Review" and its literary notices) not only kept Burke up-to-date, but involved him in a wide range of subjects. The diversity of his concerns – from economics to painting to farming – was often remarked upon, and his knowledge was far from superficial. While still at the Temple, he is reported to have engaged in conversation with a physician who was so impressed that he took Burke for a doctor and said he must be "one of the first of the faculty in Europe".

Practical expertise and an enormous range of reference were to mark Burke's public career. He knew both men and books; he understood human feelings and he did his research. When he spoke in the Commons about Ireland or America or India or France, he drew upon more than supposition; he knew what he was talking about and was able to survey the whole prospect. "His writing is magnificent," wrote his Victorian biographer John Morley, "because he knew so much, thought so comprehensively, and felt so strongly." In 1827, Lord Brougham described these talents and acquisitions:

> Possessed of much extensive knowledge, and of the most various description; acquainted alike with what different classes of men knew, each in his own province, and with much that hardly anyone ever thought of learning; he could either bring his masses of information to bear directly upon the subjects to which they severally belonged – or he could avail himself of them generally to strengthen his faculties and enlarge his views – or he could turn any portion of them to account, for the purpose of illustrating his theme or enriching his diction. Hence, when he is handling any one matter, we perceive that we are conversing with a reasoner or a teacher to whom every other branch of knowledge is familiar. His views range over all the cognate subjects; his reasonings are derived from principles applicable to other theories, as well as the one in hand. . .

About 1756, Burke began to lodge in London with an Irish doctor called Christopher Nugent, and in the spring of 1757, he married Nugent's daughter Jane, who was a practising Catholic. The marriage lasted until Burke's death, 40 years later, and was an extremely happy one. Two sons born in 1758 were named Richard and Christopher after Edmund and Jane's respective fathers, but Christopher died in infancy.

By this time, Burke was living in close association with William Burke, an adventurer and speculator whom he had met at the Temple and referred to as his "Cousin Will", though they seem not to have been close relations. In 1759, Will and Burke's brother Richard set off for the West Indies to seek their fortune. Edmund, without a secure income, applied for, but was not given, the consulship at Madrid.

Instead, he became private secretary to William Gerard Hamilton, and two years later accompanied him to Dublin when Hamilton became Chief Secretary to the Lord Lieutenant of Ireland, the Earl of Halifax. After six years of loyal labour, Burke broke with Hamilton, after writing to him to say that he could accept a proffered pension of £300 on the Irish Establishment only on the understanding that he remained free, when not working in Hamilton's interest, to pursue his own concerns. Hamilton was offended, and Burke was forced to decline the pension and leave his employment.

Back in London, he was taken up by the 2nd Marquess of Rockingham, as private secretary, and soon, by force of personality, became chief policymaker in the Whig government that Rockingham formed in July 1765. Accordingly, Burke was elected in December of that year for the pocket borough of Wendover in Buckinghamshire, and quickly distinguished himself as an orator. After his parliamentary debut, William Pitt the Elder reportedly remarked that he had "spoken in such a manner as to stop the mouths of all Europe", and added that the House should congratulate itself on the acquisition of such a Member. David Garrick was among those who sent Burke tributes of appreciation.

Burke had been a friend of Samuel Johnson's since the 1750s, and in 1764 he and his father-in-law, Dr Nugent, became founding members of Johnson's Club, along with Reynolds and Goldsmith. Since later members included Garrick, Sheridan, Boswell, Warton, Malone, Fox, Adam Smith and Sir William Jones, it must have been the greatest talking-shop ever known. Yet even in this company, Burke shone. Johnson paid tribute several times to his friend and rival in talk. On August 15, 1773, for instance, Boswell records his saying, "Burke, sir, is such a man, that if you met him for the first time in a street where you were stopped by a drove of oxen, and you and he stepped aside to take shelter but for five minutes, he'd talk to you in such a manner, that, when you parted, you would say, this is an extraordinary man."

According to *Blackwood's Magazine* in 1833, more or less this happened on one occasion in Lichfield. A clergyman in the cathedral found two strangers looking around, and offered to guide them. Later he told an acquaintance: "I have been conversing for this half-hour with a man of the most extraordinary powers of mind and extent of information which it has ever been my fortune to meet." Burke and his friend had stopped to see the town while their horses were being changed. "The clergyman's surprise was fully accounted for," the article continues, "by being told at the inn that this singular companion was Mr Burke."

In Parliament, Burke's first concern was the American question. What was to be the status of the colonies? What were their trading rights? Had Parliament a right to exact taxation, and had the colonists a right to elect Members of Parliament? Burke spoke up for conciliation, and from 1770 to 1775 he acted as agent for the New York Assembly, with a salary of £700. While conceding Parliament's hypothetical right to tax the colonists, he saw that the practical might to enforce it was lacking. New taxes, arbitrarily decided, would not carry the Americans' consent, and to seek to impose them was wrong, inexpedient and inflammatory. Parliament was pressing a principle from a position of weakness, and exacerbating rather than minimizing the disagreement. The right to tax would be self-defeating, Burke saw, if it was pressed so hard that the Americans chose independence and freed themselves from all British levies.

Furthermore, Burke wished to deflect men from talking of rights, as was increasingly the fashion, for while the British government might have rights over the colonists, the Americans might have contrary rights, and the more this language was used, the more likely a contradiction and a breach became. A better policy was for Parliament to offer concessions, to swallow its pride, and to remain on amicable terms. "The question with me is not whether you have a right to render your people miserable," he said, "but whether it is not your interest to make them happy."

This first parliamentary session was a personal triumph for Burke, and the Stamp Act was repealed, but George III dismissed Rockingham's administration in 1766, after little more than a year. Will Burke's speculations in East India stock were temporarily flourishing, and Edmund had room for manoeuvre. He was offered a place in Pitt's administration of 1766–68, but chose to remain in opposition, and was to stand loyally by Rockingham until the Marquess's death in 1782.

In 1768, Burke purchased Gregories, a Palladian house with an estate of 600 acres near Beaconsfield in Buckinghamshire, which, he was pleased to note, included the house of the poet Edmund Waller. It was to be his happy retreat for the rest of his days. The cost was in excess of £20,000, secured by two mortgages. The capital expense and annual costs were more than Burke could afford, and he was ever after in continual financial need, even though Rockingham advanced him sums estimated to total as much as £30,000. Yet Burke remained constitutionally generous. In 1765 he had borne a large part of the cost of sending the Irish painter James Barry to Italy to study, and he later rescued the poet George Crabbe from destitution and the debtors' prison. At Beaconsfield, he continued to indulge his brother Richard, as well as William Burke. He apparently credited them and his son Richard with powers comparable to his own, and the four lived and worked in such close association that a chapter in Almon's *Anecdotes* (1797) is devoted to "Messieurs Burkes".

In opposition, as he was to be for most of his parliamentary life, Burke published his *Thoughts on the Cause of the Present Discontents* (1770), which attacked George III's policy of ruling through a "court party" and making Parliament docile and submissive. In 1768, John Wilkes, the disreputable journalist and politician, had been elected for Middlesex, but was jailed for his earlier writings. From prison, he wrote accusing the Secretary of State of instigating a massacre in St George's Fields, and this was made the pretext for expelling him from the Commons. The people of Middlesex, however, continued to vote for him, placing him four times at the head of the poll, and Burke stood up for the principle that Parliament could not capriciously deprive a duly elected member of his right to sit. Everyone knew, he added, that this was really a contest between the electors and the Crown, "the Crown acting by an instrumental House of Commons". The King felt he had been insulted by Wilkes's journalism, and pursued a vendetta against him. But this was only a symptom of George's attempt to govern as well as reign, by choosing his ministers from all parties, by browbeating them, and by using patronage to secure personal adherents in every faction – known as the "King's friends" – who would always vote for his measures.

This was almost the last time a British monarch would try to assert his power in defiance of the people, and Burke was just as jealous of the rights of Parliament as the Roundheads had been 130 years before. The King's behaviour threatened the constitutional settlement of 1689. The Commons, Burke argued, did not answer to the King, but to the people. It was not the master of its constituents but their servant. The "great and only foundation of government," he wrote, was "the confidence of the people" – their consent. "The House of Commons can never be a control on other parts of government unless they are controlled themselves by their constituents; and unless these constituents possess some right in the choice of that House, which it is not in the power of that House to take away."

In this campaign, Burke showed himself a staunch advocate of the importance of the electoral principle. The constitution depended upon the Crown, the aristocracy and the commons all keeping to their proper places and not threatening one another. The present danger was of arbitrary rule; a few years later it was to be an excess of popular zeal. "Our constitution," he wrote, "stands on a nice equipoise, with steep precipices and deep water upon all sides of it." Maintaining that equipoise was ever after to be his preoccupation.

In the spring of 1771, Burke upheld a motion on the law of libel, so protecting the right of private citizens to criticize their rulers, and opposed proceedings taken by the House of Commons to prevent the publication of its debates. Together these measures helped to secure freedom of speech and free circulation of the parliamentary proceedings.

After the Boston Tea Party in 1773, Burke urged the repeal of the tea duty upon the colonists, and in March 1775 he spoke in the House for three hours, bringing forward his 13 resolutions for conciliation with America – which were, however, rejected. Undaunted, he moved a further Bill in November, arguing that "after all our struggles, our hold in America is, and must be, her good inclination. If this fails, all fails. . ." But this Bill too was thrown out.

Losing his seat at Wendover in 1774, Burke was found another by Rockingham at Malton in Yorkshire. But whilst he was dining at Malton on the day of his election, a deputation arrived from Bristol to tell him that he had been nominated there too. Bristol was then second only to London as a commercial city, so this was an honour that would enhance his status. He immediately accepted and set off for Bristol. Arriving at the mayor's house on the sixth day of the poll, he addressed the electors after only a few minutes' rest, and was triumphantly returned.

Burke was to represent Bristol for six years, but not without friction. In his remarkable, high-principled *Speech to the Electors at Bristol at the Conclusion of the Poll*, he declared that he would sit in Parliament as their representative, not as their delegate. He would always listen to his constituents' opinions, but he would not accept instructions. He owed them not his obedience, but the conscientious exercise of his faculties. This speech has become the classic statement of the role of MPs and of the integrating function of Parliament:

> Parliament is not a *congress* of ambassadors from different and hostile interests; which interests each must maintain, as an agent and advocate, against other agents and advocates; but Parliament is a *deliberative* assembly of *one* nation, with *one* interest, that of the whole; where, not local purposes, not local prejudices ought to guide, but the general good, resulting from the general reason of the whole. You choose a member indeed; but when you have chosen him, he is not a member of Bristol, but he is a Member of *Parliament*.

Burke was by now one of the most famous men of the age, but he chose not to move in fashionable society. His letters to aristocratic friends and colleagues are written with due deference (or more), but he was impatient with social occasions. In 1769 he had written to advise Barry that he must learn to humour lesser men who could afford to commission paintings, but Burke himself clearly found it hard to make urbane concessions.

In the Commons, some of his speeches were excessively long and were met with impatience or barracking. Additionally, he found his character and background under frequent attack in the press. His calls for relaxation of restrictions on Irish trade and of the laws against Catholics eventually cost him the support of the merchants of his Bristol constituency. When Parliament was dissolved in September 1780, he went to Bristol to explain his principles and actions, but after two days' canvassing found he stood no chance of re-election, and so declined to stand. From then until his retirement in 1794 he represented Malton.

With the loss of America, after Cornwallis's surrender to Washington at Yorktown in October 1781, the ministry of Lord North, first formed in 1770, was seen to have failed, and North resigned the following spring. Now, at last, Rockingham began his second administration, but still he failed to bring the man who was the driving force of the Whigs into the Cabinet. Instead, Burke became Paymaster General of the Forces, at £4,000 a year, and a Privy Counsellor. His son, Richard, became his deputy, at £500 a year; his brother became Secretary to the Treasury, at £3,000 a year, and Will Burke was given a place in India under the Pay Office. In his *Speech on Economical Reform* in 1780, Burke had proposed abolition of many sinecures in the royal household. His intention had been to limit the Crown's scope for unconstitutional influence through jobbery and corruption, and to secure the independence of the Commons. Now, in office, he pushed through a new Bill, considerably weakened, but nevertheless abolishing 134 posts in the royal household and civil administration. The Bill also, to Burke's personal cost, put an end to the custom of private profiteering by the Paymaster General.

In July 1782, after only three months in office, Rockingham died, and the administration broke up. There followed the ministry of another Whig, Lord Shelburne, whom Burke heartily detested. With both Burke and his protege Charles James Fox refusing to serve under him, Shelburne was forced to resign early in 1783, to be succeeded by an unlikely coalition, which had the Duke of Portland at its head, and included North, Fox and Burke (again at the Pay Office).

For two years, Burke had been part of a select committee upon Indian affairs. Eleven reports were presented to Parliament, some of them Burke's unaided work. Together they revealed the depravity of the East India Company's regime under Warren Hastings, who had been distrusted by Burke since before he was appointed Governor-General of Bengal in 1773. Now Burke drew up an East India Bill to curtail the powers of the Company by handing over the administration of India to a government commission of seven appointees. The Bill was introduced into the Commons by Fox, but backed by an impassioned and vastly detailed speech by Burke against the iniquities of the Company's rule.

The Bill passed comfortably in the Commons, but there were

huge vested interests against it in the country, and the King – who was anxious to dispense with the coalition – saw his chance. Acting unconstitutionally, he put pressure on the Lords, who duly threw it out in December. The ministry was now dismissed in favour of the Tories. Burke was never again to hold office, and the Whigs were to remain in opposition for the rest of the century. At the beginning of 1784, the 25-year-old William Pitt the Younger, who had been in Parliament only since 1781, became Prime Minister, virtually for the rest of his short life.

Burke, however, was not deflected from his purpose. At length, in 1787, he argued successfully that Warren Hastings, who had been consistently contemptuous of the very lives of the Indian people, should be impeached for exceeding his powers and for high crimes and misdemeanours. So was instigated one of the most prolonged legal proceedings ever known. The case was to dominate much of the rest of Burke's life. He made his first speech as chief manager of the impeachment in Westminster Hall in 1788, and his last in 1794. His campaign against this injustice lasted in all more than 15 years, and was fired by an unmatched, unabating moral indignation. It was for this, he wrote, that he valued himself most.

In his *Speech on the Nabob of Arcot's Debts* (1785), which occupies more than 120 octavo pages in his works, he unravelled a byzantine conspiracy of scarcely credible audacity by which Parliament had been defrauded, and showed that the workings of the East India Company were systematically corrupt. In the event, Hastings was acquitted by a few exhausted peers, but Burke's campaign spelt an end to the hegemony of the Company which had "begun in commerce and ended in empire". John Morley later wrote that Burke laid the foundations "once for all of a moral, just, philanthropic and responsible public opinion in England with reference to India, and in so doing performed perhaps the most magnificent service that any statesman has ever had it in his power to render to humanity". P. J. Marshall, who is editing the Indian volumes of Burke's *Writings and Speeches*, is less sure of Burke's effect on events, but concludes that as the "self-appointed conscience of British India", he left behind him "an uncompromising statement of the priority of moral principles that applied not only to India but to all government".

Meanwhile in France, the year 1789 saw peaceful reform turn to bloody revolution, and Burke began to fear that the contagion would spread from "that very neighbouring nation which the other day I could see so clearly from the pier of Ramsgate". Just as the capricious violence in India had roused him to prosecute Hastings, so the lawlessness of the French mob persuaded him to take up his pen against the revolution. His *Reflections on the Revolution in France, and on the Proceedings in Certain Societies in London relative to that Event*, published in November 1790, sold some 17,000 copies in two months, and was soon acclaimed throughout Europe. But it was also attacked by many who saw in the revolution the breaking out of a new spirit of freedom. The most important of the responses was Thomas Paine's *Rights of Man* (1791), and between them these two books have ever since been taken to define the politics of conservatism and progressivism.

Burke was thought by many to have gone too far in condemning the French Revolution, towards which many leading Whigs were favourable to begin with. On May 6, 1791, in one of the greatest emotional scenes ever witnessed in the Commons, he publicly broke with Fox, the Whig leader and his friend of 25 years. In a debate nominally about the Quebec Bill, Burke began to denounce the new French Constitution and "the horrible consequences flowing from the French idea of the rights of man". Fox accused him of speaking out of order, and repeated his own admiration for the revolution. Burke now found himself shouted down by many on his own side of the House. Yet he insisted:

> It certainly was indiscreet at any period, but especially at his time of life, to parade enemies, or give his friends occasion to desert him; yet if his firm and steady adherence to the British constitution placed him in such a dilemma, he would risk all, and, as public duty and public experience taught him, with his last words exclaim, "Fly from the French Constitution."

Here, Fox whispered that there was "no loss of friends". But Burke said "Yes, there was a loss of friends – he knew the price of his conduct – he had done his duty at the price of his friend, their friendship was at an end."

Burke was now accused by the newspapers and caricaturists of inconsistency, of going over to the Tories, and of seeking favour with the King. Shortly afterwards, he published *An Appeal from the*

New to the Old Whigs, written in the third person, in which he defended his consistency:

> He who thinks that the British constitution ought to consist of the three members, of three very different natures, of which it does actually consist, and thinks it his duty to preserve each of those members in its proper place, and with its proper proportion of power, must (as each shall happen to be attacked) vindicate the three several parts on the several principles peculiarly belonging to them. He cannot assert the democratic part on the principles on which monarchy is supported; nor can he support monarchy on the principles of democracy. . .

The overarching principle was that many principles are needed. For the rest of his life Burke was to oppose reconciliation with France as long as its leaders were propagating a unified theory which he considered homicidal, regicidal and suicidal.

Pitt was reluctant to go to war, but in Janaury 1793 Louis XVI was executed, and in February France declared war on Britain. Burke knew it would be a long war, but urged Pitt, for the sake of the balance of power, not to break up the territory of France. He also wished the government to proclaim that Britain was at war not with the French nation, but with what he called its "*armed doctrine*". Pitt did not at first grasp the importance of the distinction, but by June 7, 1799, he was echoing Burke, saying: "We are at war with armed opinions".

For Burke, 1794 was filled with grief. In February, his brother Richard, with whom he had shared his home, his thoughts and the burden of the Hastings impeachment, died. With a final nine-day speech on the case, Burke closed his parliamentary career, and retired. But there was no well-earned relief. On August 2, his hope for the future was extinguished with the death from tuberculosis of his son Richard, who at 36 had been elected a fortnight previously to take over Burke's seat in Parliament. The bereaved father was inconsolable, and virtually a broken man, although for three years he continued to publish his vigorous, plaintive opinions on French affairs. He died on July 9, 1797, and lies buried in the church at Beaconsfield.

3

Constancy and Consistency

While the French Revolution was in its infancy, Burke recognized it as the crucial event of modern history. It changed everything and began a new epoch. The ideas and effects of the revolution still dominate liberal thought. Most of the political pieties and rhetoric of today would have sounded familiar to Burke, and he would have been able to say exactly why these ideas have failed, over two centuries, to produce the benefits they promised. He considered "this great revolution in human affairs" – which extended "even to the constitution of the mind of man" – to be a profound and evil mistake. It was "the greatest moral earthquake that ever convulsed and shattered this globe of ours", and "the most important crisis that ever existed in the world".

The revolutionaries did not disagree about its scope. They congratulated themselves on beginning the world anew, according to rational theories. They dismissed, as Burke put it, "the ancient permanent sense of mankind", and asserted that it had failed. For them, the new Enlightenment meant the end of a dark age – from which they thought nothing positive could be learnt. The new start in France was marked by a new calendar, beginning the world again at year one. The intention was to achieve the most complete historical disjunction.

"The present age will hereafter merit to be called the Age of Reason," wrote Paine in *The Rights of Man*, "and the present generation will appear to the future as the Adam of a new world." Encouraged by the century's advances in knowledge, he and many others thought the organization of society ought to be amenable to the simple force of reason, extrapolating from nature. Just as Descartes had wished to begin with the fewest possible preconceptions – from "Cogito, ergo sum" – so the revolutionaries believed they could build a society from pure enlightened thought shorn of the superstitions of the ages. Joseph Priestley wrote that there had been "a change from darkness to light, from superstition to sound knowledge . . . a liberating of all the powers of man from that variety of fetters by which they have hitherto been held."

Such claims were quickly ridiculed, and the term "enlightenment" was used sarcastically of the French Encyclopaedists by the French themselves. *The Oxford English Dictionary* records uses of the word "to designate the spirit and aims of the French philosophers of the 18th century, or of others whom it is intended to associate with them in the implied charge of shallow and pretentious intellectualism, unreasonable contempt for tradition and authority, etc." The Dictionary's first citation is from 1865, but the spirit of Burke infuses its definition, and he had begun the attack long before, in November 1789, in one of his earliest pronouncements on the revolution. In a letter to Charles-Jean-François Depont, he warned, bitterly, that his opinions were not all to the taste of "this enlightened age; and, indeed, are no better than the late ripe fruit of mere experience". Doubtless he and his French correspondent were both aware that the term *lumières* was already in use ironically. In another letter of the time Burke rounds upon the terminology of the new visionaries, writing plainly that their grand project "carries evident marks of the incurable ignorance of this most unenlightened age". In the *Reflections*, he writes that "if the word 'enlightened' be understood according to the new dictionary," it means not believing in God – or, by extension, in all that Burke considered to be God-given.

Burke castigated both the French Revolution and the philosophy behind it. He did not believe that "nature" – the great frame of the world and of man, to which the revolutionaries appealed – was transparent and straightforward, as they pretended. Complex, half-hidden and half-understood, it was instead mediated to men and women in many ways. "Those habits which are communicated by the circumstances of civil life," he wrote, amount to a "second nature", and it is that which is our proper element. So he scorned the attempt to replace sophisticated institutions, hard-won political accommodations and even long-observed habits with utopian slogans and sentimental appeals.

Showing the devastating contradictions inherent in the revolutionaries' hopes, he warned of the longer-term effects of disturbing the people's "unsuspecting confidence" in their situation by asking questions to which there might be no answers – or perhaps only answers beyond the present comprehension or beyond the common man. "He never had loved, and never should love an abstract question," the *Parliamentary History* reports him saying in the Commons, "being of opinion that much of the vice of the present age was owing to an abstract way of thinking" (*PH*, XXVIII, 1031). His writings predicted many of our dissatisfactions, because he saw the vulnerability of the abstractions on which our tottering modern political edifice has been built.

Yet Burke's greatness was not merely as a conservative who valued tradition as "the collective wisdom of mankind". He was also – and firstly – a pioneer of humanitarian and liberal reform. In the age of William Wilberforce and John Howard (whose humane prison work Burke vociferously supported), and a generation before the great reforms of social and working conditions, he was urging religious tolerance and an end to the cruel laws of debt, which required payment before prisoners could be released but offered them no means to earn money. He also devoted many years to impeaching "the great delinquent", Warren Hastings, for crimes against humanity in India.

When Burke opposed the French Revolution, many contemporaries were astonished. He had, after all, made common cause with the radical Thomas Paine over Britain's unjust treatment of the Americans (though the two men acted on quite different planes and principles); and during the Wilkes fiasco he had written at length about the importance of maintaining the independent representative function of the Commons and reducing the power of the King. The great 20th-century Burke scholar T. W. Copeland describes his record:

> Burke had been in politics for over thirty years at the time the Revolution began, and almost every major effort of his career had been reform in one shape or another. Against the bitter opposition of George III and the "King's friends" he had put through his Bill for Economical Reform in the early 1780s – probably the most important single act of reform achieved in England in the eighteenth century. Against an even more determined "Indian interest" he was struggling in the late 'eighties to reform the administration of British India. He had fought against the misgovernment of Ireland, against the African slave trade, against the oppression of

> Catholics and dissenters, against the imprisonment of debtors. There were very few causes of reform agitated in that day in which Burke had not taken a leading and effective part.
>
> (*Edmund Burke: Six Essays.*)

The public knew Burke as a reformer and a liberal, and mistook the French Revolution for a liberal cause. But after his battles over Ireland, America and India, Burke realized at once that the revolution was an aberration and a wrong turning for liberalism, the Whigs and the world. "French liberty", he declared, "is nothing but the rein given to vice and confusion."

In 1790, he could justly claim in the last paragraph of *Reflections on the Revolution in France* that almost the whole of his public exertion had been "a struggle for the liberty of others" and an attempt to "discredit opulent oppression", yet that book shows how these principles are served not by upheaval, but by extension of a civil society. He believed not in unrestrained individualism, but in a corporate, social liberty. "Liberty", he had told the Sheriffs of Bristol twelve years before, "must be limited in order to be possessed." A free government was one that could "temper together" the "opposite elements of liberty and restraint in one consistent work". This avoided the twin dangers of anarchy and its product, tyranny.

Burke rejoiced to live in "freedom under a qualified monarchy". The phrase comes from the pivotal year of 1789 (again from the letter to Charles-Jean-François Depont), but Burke might have used those words at any date. For although his energies were sometimes expended on maintaining the qualifications on royal power, and at other times on maintaining the monarchy itself, a balanced freedom was always his overriding aim. In the letter, Burke challenges the loose understanding of the term "liberty". What he thinks men entitled to

> is not solitary, unconnected, individual, selfish liberty, as if every man was to regulate the whole of his conduct by his own will. The liberty I mean is *social* freedom. It is that state of things in which liberty is secured by the equality of restraint; a constitution of things in which the liberty of no one man, and no body of men, and no number of men, can find means to trespass on the liberty of any person, or any description of persons, in the society. This kind of liberty is, indeed, but another name for justice; ascertained by wise laws, and secured by well-constructed institutions.

And among the bodies of men that must not be allowed to trespass on the people's liberty, he included the government. For he understood what the French revolutionaries soon began to find to their cost: that the state could be the most virulent and arbitrary of the forces that destroy freedom.

The nation that secured its liberty while yet securing its strength was to be envied, and this Burke believed Britain had achieved. How it had been done had long been his study. Explaining it was to be the task of the remainder of his life, the late ripe fruit of his extensive experience. For in Britain, "the grand secret had been found, of reconciling a government of real energy for all foreign and all domestic purposes, with the most perfect security to the liberty and safety of individuals." That secret was the mixed constitution.

Burke's mature conception of Britain's "*compound constitution*" challenges today's politics as simplistic and monocular. For the constitution that he tried to uphold was a pragmatic balance of contending powers, with monarchy, aristocracy and commons restraining each other – at once "balanced as opposing interests" and yet "also connected as friends". As it has been handed on to us, Britain's unwritten constitution retains vestiges of this ideal, but scarcely anyone now appears to believe in balancing democracy with more stable powers, and many of those most active in political thinking wish to end what they consider infringements of the sovereignty of the people.

In describing the mixed constitution, Burke was but the most profound and eloquent writer and statesman of his time. He did not, he said, "aim at singularity". The British had appreciated the ideal in other ages and places long before it was achieved at home. Bruce Redford has found that from the end of the 16th century British visitors to Venice dwelt on the enduring success of the republic's mixed constitution. This embodied principles which, in Redford's words in his *Venice and the Grand Tour*, had been "adumbrated by Aristotle and analysed by Polybius: the ideal polity is that which distributes power amongst the elements of the one, the few, and the many, thereby achieving a harmonious blend of monarchy, aristocracy, and democracy". As if symbolically, the Venetian Republic came to an eventual end with the invasion of the rampaging French in the year of Burke's death, 1797.

In his "General Observations on the Fall of the Roman Empire in the West", published in 1781, Edward Gibbon explains that "the deep foundations of the greatness of Rome" had also consisted of a mixed constitution: "The temperate struggles of the patricians and plebians had finally established the firm and equal balance of the constitution; which united the freedom of popular assemblies, with the authority and wisdom of a senate, and the executive powers of a regal magistrate." Gibbon would have expected his British readers to bless their good fortune in living in a country that had achieved a similar balance, based on Charles I's *Answer to the XIX Propositions*, June 18, 1642, which declared that the British constitution was a mixed one:

> There being three kinds of government among men, absolute monarchy, aristocracy and democracy, and all these having their particular conveniences and inconveniences, the experience and wisdom of your ancestors hath so moulded this out of a mixture of these acts as to give to this kingdom (as far as human prudence can contrive) the conveniences of all three, without the inconveniences of any one, as long as the balance hangs even between the three estates. . .
>
> (cit. *The Stuart Constitution*, ed. Kenyon)

This then was the orthodoxy, and there was by the late 18th century a cross-party satisfaction with the lineaments of the constitution. As Samuel Taylor Coleridge said on January 28, 1832,

> The ideal Tory and the ideal Whig (and some such there have really been), agreed in the necessity and benefit of an exact balance of the three estates: but the Tory was more jealous of the balance being deranged by the people; the Whig, of its being deranged by the Crown. But this was a habit, a jealousy only; they both agreed in the ultimate preservation of the balance; and accordingly they might each, under certain circumstances, without the slightest inconsistency, pass from one side to the other, as the ultimate object required it. This the Tories did at the [Glorious] Revolution, but remained Tories as before.
>
> (*Table Talk.*)

Burke would have resisted any inference from Coleridge's phrase about an "exact balance of the three estates" that the monarchy, and the Houses of Lords and Commons should always be equal, or that no one of them should exercise untrammelled power in some matters. He was a proud guardian, for instance, of the Commons' exclusive right to control the national finances. The three balancing estates were distinct and distinctive powers, comprehensive only when they worked together.

> The whole scheme of our mixed constitution is to prevent any one of its principles from being carried as far, as taken by itself, and theoretically, it would go. . . To avoid the perfections of extreme, all its several parts are so constituted as not alone to answer their own several ends, but also each to limit and control the others. . .
>
> (*Appeal to the Old Whigs.*)

So although Burke pondered it more deeply than anyone, the three-in-one constitution – which may also have derived strength from the Christian doctrine of the Trinity – was widely accepted. His exceptional and prescient ability was to see how the balance was tipping. His fear was always that change would allow one of the estates of the realm permanently to overwhelm the others. Like Coleridge, he regarded the Glorious Revolution of 1688 as having been a necessary measure to thwart an overweening monarch, and the Act of Settlement as the triumphant legal means by which the constitutional balance had been restored. But a century after that English Revolution came the crisis of the French Revolution, which threatened that British balance and settlement. Charles James Fox had in his early career also wished to maintain the "equipoise" of the three estates, but in the face of the French Revolution, the Whig leader supposed that the threat was once again from an over-powerful monarchy. However, Burke – who in 1780 had supported the famous resolution that the influence of the Crown had increased, was increasing and ought to be diminished – realized that on the contrary this time it was the people, little understanding what they were doing, who were endangering the equilibrium. "In the last age," he proclaimed in his *Speech on the Army Estimates* (1790), "we were in danger of being entangled by the example of France in the net of a relentless despotism. It is not necessary to say anything upon that example. It exists no longer. Our present danger from the example of a people whose character knows no medium, is, with regard to government, a danger from anarchy."

Burke was never on the side of the monarchy or of the people *per se*, nor did he want to see them at odds. He was adamant in his conviction that each had entitlements, duties and particular qualities, and that these could be maintained only in a balance that sustained both. In the *Reflections*, he denounces the "old fanatics of single arbitrary power" as well as the fanatics of democracy. He stood at the pivot, throwing his weight on one side then the other as circumstances required. In his early essay *Thoughts on the Present Discontents*, and as a leading light in Lord Rockingham's opposition in the late 1760s, he denounced George III's attempts to impose his will on Parliament by operating a party of courtiers. Yet in 1789, he supported the monarchy in France.

Often in his lifetime Burke was accused of inconsistency, as he still is occasionally today. In the grand closing sentence of the *Reflections*, he rebuts the charge, writing that he was one who "would preserve consistency by varying his means to secure the unity of his end". Circumstances had changed, but his principles had not. And these principles are of permanent value, although their application varies. Even Michael Freeman, who delights to find Burke "far from consistent", concedes as much:

> It is a vulgar error to suppose that Burke was guilty of inconsistency because he supported the 1689 and American revolutions and opposed the French. It is a vulgar error partly because he supported the American revolution with extreme caution (he supported the American *cause* rather than the American *revolution*). It is also a vulgar error because, in his views of these three revolutions, Burke maintained the same set of general principles. In his attitude towards 1689 and 1776, he was never a radical.
>
> (*Edmund Burke and the Critique of Political Radicalism*.)

Burke was, as he wrote of himself in his *Appeal to the Old Whigs*, "supposed to have passed from extreme to extreme; but he has always kept himself in a medium. This charge is not so wonderful. It is in the nature of things, that they who are in the centre of a circle should appear directly opposed to those who view them from any part of the circumference." This remark may appear egocentric, but a close examination of his record shows that Burke maintained himself within a series of working principles. The man once regarded as liberal may now be wrongly thought of as a last-ditch reactionary, but even his detractors should acknowledge that he would have argued that today's liberals are the extremists. He would have considered Britain's modern domestic political arrangements as a victory for unmitigated democracy, and as such a ruination of the equipollence that he struggled to maintain.

In his *Biographia Literaria* (1817), Coleridge paid this tribute to Burke's grounded opinions:

> . . . that man deserves the esteem of his countrymen, even as patriots, who devotes his life and the utmost efforts of his intellect to the preservation and continuance of that unanimity [grounded on moral feelings] by the disclosure and establishment of *principles*. For by these all *opinions* must be ultimately tried; and (as the feelings of men are worthy of regard only as far as they are the representatives of their fixed opinions), on the knowledge of these all unanimity not accidental and fleeting must be grounded. Let the scholar who doubts this assertion refer only to the speeches and writings of EDMUND BURKE at the commencement of the American war and compare them with his speeches and writings at the commencement of the French Revolution. He will find the *principles* exactly the same and the deductions the same; but the practical inferences almost opposite in the one case from those drawn in the other; yet in both equally legitimate and in both equally confirmed by the results. Whence gained he this superiority of foresight? . . . How are we to explain the notorious fact that the speeches and writings of EDMUND BURKE are more interesting at the present day than they were found at the time of their first publication? . . . Not only the debates in Parliament, not only our proclamations and state papers, but the essays and leading paragraphs of our journals are so many remembrancers of EDMUND BURKE.

4

Progress

Three years later, in a letter of April 8, 1820, to Thomas Allsop, Coleridge writes of "the contest between the two great moving principles of social humanity – religious adherence to the past and the ancient, the desire and the admiration of permanence, on the one hand; and the passion for increase of knowledge, for truth as the offspring of reason, in short, the mighty instincts of *Progression* and *Free-agency*, on the other", and says they are "necessary each to the continued existence of the other". By reputation now, Burke is undoubtedly the representative of the first of these principles, because he is known almost exclusively for his greatest work, the *Reflections*, which was provoked by the greatest crisis of his lifetime – an example of the second principle, of *Progression* and *Free-agency* unrestrained. Carried away by this radical principle, the time needed to be reminded of its opposite. And the case is the same today. Of the two dangers, our society is closer to the Charybdis of chaos than to the Scylla of immovable adherence to the past. Which is why Burkean reminders of a more settled age are still needed.

A sober and steady confidence in liberty was in Burke's time being superseded by the worship of progress – a notion of continuous movement in one direction, becoming more and more extended and extreme. The emblem of such movement is the ratchet. Burke's own reputation exemplifies this. As a Whig, he belonged to the more reformist of the two parties, but in 1795 he writes that his party "has long taken leave of me". During the 19th century, his ideas were seen as basic to the foundations of the Conservative Party, but as Conservativism in turn compromised with socialism after 1945, they began to be considered ultra-right-wing. His ideas have indisputably not changed since 1797, but "progress" has shifted the political triangulation points.

Yet despite enormous economic growth and material gain since Burke's day, "the progressive movement" which John Stuart Mill called "the boast of the modern world" has led not towards harmony and satisfaction, but away from them, to one trauma upon another. In one of the richest and most progressive nations on earth, the United States, enormous numbers of people are given counselling for ever-increasing numbers of complaints stemming from the problems of indisciplined freedom, from the injustices of being incompletely happy and from the very condition of being alive. The longing for "progress" militates against contentment with one's lot. When it leads to personal initiative and ambition, it is to be welcomed; often, though, it leads to envy, grudges and despair, which harm individual lives and are even more damaging when turned against society.

One terrible result of the mentality of "progress" has been to give politics almost unlimited pretensions and presumptions. It is forever seeking to achieve this or that, rather than passively holding the ring. Politicians feel they cannot leave people to live as they will, but must be cajoling them, legislating, announcing targets, initiatives and programmes. Worse, they feel obliged to "attack" this, that and one another. They see everything in terms of problems to be solved, and are loath to accept that some hardships or enmities may be perennial, even ingrained in human nature, and so beyond their capabilities. Naïvely they suppose that a conflict such as that in Northern Ireland has a narrowly political "solution".

In Burke's day, ordinary MPs were not paid, and politics, for most of them, was informed and kept in perspective by other activities; now they are professionals, driven by personal ambition and obsessed with tactical manoeuvring. Their projects, unfortunately, impinge upon private life, because government is by nature compulsory. And because politicians must be doing, there is a class of person without convictions for whom politics is a superior kind of soap-opera or fashion-parade in which the comings and goings are in themselves glamorous and entertaining.

Among radicals, "progress" has no agreed goal. Instead of a destination, it invokes an ever-receding destiny, the end of the rainbow. Its only end is itself. No particular outcome could satisfy the restlessness of a radicalism that mistakes momentum for purpose. Radicalism is not a programme, but a proselytizing discontent, ever alert for new injustices, some of which are conspicuously trumped up. The Younger Pitt described the agitators of the 18th century in words that might have been taken from Burke, and which still apply. It was the peculiar object of Jacobinism, he said, "to avail itself of every cause of discontent, to operate upon the sufferings, the prejudices, the passions or the errors of every man in the country". Although the term was not used until the 20th century, the era of militancy as a political way of life had begun.

"Progress" does not seek a potential satisfaction and stasis, but feeds on dissatisfaction and resentment, which, therefore, it must stoke. A surly trade union leader interviewed on television showed a mastery of the technique when she claimed that giving service, in a shop for instance, was quite unacceptable, because it meant being servile and demeaning oneself. Instead, staff and customers should enter negotiations on equal terms. On first hearing, this sounds ludicrous, but if it is repeated and repeated, workers will stop taking pride in being helpful and being valued by their customers, and will begin to feel exploited and resentful. Service will join the expanding lexicon of dirty words, and gradually a whole new kettle of discontents can be brought to the boil.

The idea of "human rights", similarly, is being extended by the cooking up of what would once have been dismissed as a joke: "animal rights". And the latest enlargement of this in turn is the idea that we must not discriminate against animals by using expressions that take their names in vain, such as "bitch", "catty" or "male chauvinist pig". A radical writes: "Particularly amiable and sensitive, pigs possess none of the sexist's ugly character traits. . ." (Particularly unsound, that discriminating "Particularly", as though some animals were less amiable and sensitive – but these thought police are still being trained.) So we shall have to censor *King Lear*, with its "sharper than a serpent's tooth", "detested kite", "wolvish visage" and so forth. It seems a high price to pay just to be equal with a dog, a horse, a rat. This is the doctrine of equality run mad, as grievance-mongers look for one unsuspected discrimination after another. The trick is to alert the gullible to ways in which they are being oppressed that they have never previously noticed. People are then doubly indignant, because they feel they have been not only victims but dupes as well. Counselling, court cases and legislation then follow. A classic of this genre of synthetic outrage was printed in *The Times* several years ago after the paper had said that trade unions were being treated like lepers by the government. Next day, sure enough, there it was, a letter of complaint: this was grossly unfair to lepers. . .

Campaigns such as these against various perceived injustices or for various kinds of equality and indiscrimination have a tendency to become fanatical. Animal rights protesters, for instance, start to believe that it is just to endanger or sacrifice human life for the sake of their cause. People are indoctrinated with the idea that they are taking part in an irresistible struggle, and that history will vindicate whatever they may do. When they find they cannot prevail by argument, they resort to violence and terrorism. As Burke wrote, "a controversial zeal soon turns its thoughts on force". And zeal leads on to new extremes.

The history of the French Revolution demonstrated how each generation of "progressives" is liable to be denounced as having betrayed the cause as soon as it tries to achieve a new equilibrium. As early as September 1789, Burke was writing in a letter that the National Assembly would not be free to deliberate, "as there is a mob of their constituents ready to hang them if they should deviate into moderation".

As Pierre Vergniaud, the leader of the Girondists, said in March 1793 (seven months before he was guillotined), the revolution went on "successively devouring its children". Burke explained why: "By what they call reasoning without prejudice, they leave not one stone upon another in the fabric of human society. They subvert all the authority which they hold, as well as all that which they have destroyed." The leaders failed to set themselves up as trustees of the revolution, because the revolution was antipathetic to trusteeship.

Abstract social improvements are easy to argue for, because there is a lot wrong with the world. People are delighted to see a vision of a new earth where the grass is greener and life is fairer. A scheme of progress, triumph and felicity holds out an Elysian prospect. And because people know so well the frustrations and shortcomings of this life, they assume that major changes will be beneficial, and that they will be the beneficiaries. Seeing the cracks in a theoretical edifice is impossible, for in theory there are none. Or as Burke has it, "No difficulties occur in what has never been tried." Seeing the achievements and blessings of what we actually enjoy is much harder, since these are taken for granted. There is in mankind an "unfortunate propensity", Burke wrote, "to the finding and exaggerating faults". Any literary or artistic critic knows that it is easier to see flaws and to carp than to find adequate terms of appreciation.

During the French Revolution, the extreme radicals believed that the world could be not just improved but perfected. "Perfectibility is one of the most unequivocal characteristics of the human species," wrote William Godwin in his *Political Justice* (1793), where he went on to argue that pure rationalism could take the place of government and even of such institutions as marriage. "The spirit of free and rational enquiry is now abroad", wrote Joseph Priestley in his *Letters to Edmund Burke* (1791), "and without any aid from the powers of this world, will not fail to overturn all error, and false religion, wherever it is found. . ."

The dreams of such system-builders will always be more beautiful than the mundane world we inhabit – otherwise no one would dream them. Their true fault lies not in internal incoherence, but simply in their being dreams and theories. They are not real. When in 1772 the Abbé Sieyès wrote that "true political science is the science not of *what is*, but of *what ought to be*", he made the classic mistake. Science is about knowing, not dreaming. This was a man who when asked for directions would say, "I wouldn't start from here." More practical men see that the pursuit of millennial hopes may exact too high a price in terms of actually established goods. In the words of the preface to the Prayer Book, "common experience showeth, that where a change hath been made of things advisedly established (no evident necessity so requiring) sundry inconveniences have thereupon ensued; and those many times more and greater than the evils, that were intended to be remedied by such change". And when the change is destructive and the benefit uncertain, the case is all the stronger. "I confess to you", wrote Burke in a letter, "that I have no great opinion of that sublime abstract, metaphysic reversionary, contingent humanity, which in *cold blood* can subject the *present time*, and those whom we *daily see and converse with*, to *immediate* calamities in favour of the future and uncertain benefit of persons who *only exist in idea*."

Burke felt a particular contempt for the kind of self-appointed, self-validating claques who claim to represent a public desire for thoroughgoing reforms. In *Observations on the Conduct of the Minority* (written 1793), he warns that the danger from groups such as the Revolution Society (then) or Charter 88 (now) is that "without legal names, these clubs will be led to assume political capacities; that they may debate the forms of the constitution; and that from their meetings they may insolently dictate their will to the regular authorities of the kingdom, in the manner in which the Jacobin clubs issue their mandates to the National Assembly. . ." Exactly this process is at work when opposition parties set up a quasi-official commission to investigate the constitutional position of Scotland or Northern Ireland. The constitutional position is known: they are part of the United Kingdom. But when such a body begins to talk of a Scottish parliament, and to decide where this fiction might sit, it is presumptuously attempting to change the constitution without any authority. The danger is that the talk may prove self-fulfilling, because newspapers and broadcasters take such bodies, and such fictions, at their own estimation. Journalists have a reckless and unaccountable influence over such matters, and an inherent interest in change, because it is news.

In one of the funniest metaphors in the *Reflections*, Burke warns his French friend against taking agitators to be representative of the general opinion:

> The vanity, restlessness, petulance, and spirit of intrigue of several petty cabals, who attempt to hide their total want of consequence in bustle and noise, and puffing, and mutual quotation of each other, makes you imagine that our contemptuous neglect of their abilities is a mark of general acquiescence in their opinions. No such thing, I assure you. Because half a dozen grasshoppers under a fern make the field ring with their importunate chink, whilst thousands of great cattle, reposed beneath the shadow of the British oak, chew the cud and are silent, pray do not imagine that those who make the noise are the only inhabitants of the field; that of course, they are many in number; or that, after all, they are other than the little shrivelled, meagre, hopping, though loud and troublesome insects of the hour.

These masterly sentences not only mock the shrillness of supporters of the Revolution Society, but demonstrate the placid power and weight of the settled, contemplative majority. The agitators are busily puffing one another (always with the risk that the balloon will burst). Like crickets talkin' back and forth in rhyme, they resort not only to "mutual quotation", but to mutual quotation, emphatically, "of each other" – as if platitudes might improve by repetition. But though they in their squeaking laugh contemn, these are but insects. Their doctrines are slight, fragile and shortlived, in contrast to the long-established principles of tenancy. The true occupants, the great somnolent cattle, need only swish their tails. In reply to Burke's first, 52-word sentence about the cabalists, six words of brisk dismissal suffice: "No such thing, I assure you."

And yet over and over again, the discontents have it. The commotion of the dreamers and schemers is evident and draws them together; those resistant to change tend to remain silent, isolated and uncounted. So the progressive fallacy continues to be played out to its disastrous conclusion. A particularly harmful example, fully in the spirit of 1789, was the systematic dismantling of British education under the name of "comprehensivization". The ugliness of the word should have been warning enough. Nonetheless, twenty years after escaping the horrors of totalitarianism, Britain embarked on comprehensivism. Not content to improve or renovate schools by following the best models, governments built upon the sands of an untried theory. Schools were closed or converted, and traditional practice was treated with contempt. The inherited and practical experience of teachers was ignored. Had grammar schools been working effectively since Shakespeare's day? Did pupils and local people have affection and loyalty for them? Then close them: they must not compete with the visionary new establishments. Did streaming of pupils enable more focused teaching? Did it save both the intelligent and the dull from embarrassment? Then abolish it in favour of mixed-ability classes. Did school uniform give a sense of belonging? Then scrap it. Was the teaching of Latin helpful when it came to the writing of English? Condemn it.

There were problems with the existing schools provision, and it could have been improved by local changes and comparison of methods. The reformers had before them the example of one of the oldest and most academically successful of educational networks: the grammar schools. Furthermore, many in government and the civil service had been educated privately, in the leading schools in the world. But did they distil their experience and replicate the best? They did not. The educational theorists knew better than the educators. They thought they could teach the teachers a thing or two. They hadn't the humility to acknowledge that after several centuries of practice, Winchester College might have discovered something about educating children, or Manchester Grammar School be able to offer a few basic rules. As Burke wrote of the French revolutionaries, "in these gentlemen there is nothing of the tender parental solicitude which fears to cut up the infant for the sake of an experiment".

When Matthew Arnold advocated state schools in 1861, he had in mind seats of learning that would rival the best: "Such schools would soon prove notable competitors with the existing public schools; they would do these a great service by stimulating them, and making them look into their weak points more closely." Comprehensives never managed – or even tried – to compete. The public schools have felt they have nothing to gain from the deliberately perverse methods of comprehensives. On the contrary, a former headmaster of Eton has stated – too late, too late – that if mixed-ability teaching worked, the public schools would practise it.

The effects of this wholesale revolution are painful to rehearse and now widely recognized. Many present-day pupils in Britain learn less than Burke did at his Irish hedge school. The educational revolution was certainly comprehensive. Where once the secondary modern schools may have relegated many children to second-class educational status, the comprehensives now manage to relegate far larger numbers in the name of equality. And so, as the nation finally tries to clear up the mess which includes unprecedented numbers of children with "special needs" and wildly escalating numbers with no school to go to after expulsion, there is scarcely a model of state schooling to revive. After 30 years, thousands of teachers, having come through such schools themselves, know nothing but the comprehensive orthodoxies and are bewildered by the increasing contempt and violence of their pupils. The tradition of proper schooling has all but gone. The need for a return to some basic precepts is now recognized, and they will have to be recovered; but who is to teach grammar, for instance, when so few understand it? Increasing numbers of adults are angry about their own "liberal" education, because they have found from experience how ignorant it left them. But in many places the living tradition of teaching and learning has been broken.

Radical change tends to throw away incidental advantages in the established arrangements which are not recognized until they are gone. But change that is abrupt rather than gradual or imperceptible has further drawbacks: to effect it completely may require compulsion, for it is unlikely to carry the consent of all the people. Disregarding old loyalties, it gives them no time to wither away. On the contrary, by insulting those people who remain loyal to the previous regimen, a sudden innovation is liable to make them implacable. Henry VIII's rejection of the authority of the Pope and the dissolution of the monasteries were followed by protracted religious paranoia and persecution; the establishment of a republic after the execution of Charles I did not extinguish loyalty to the monarchy, and the restoration 11 years later was highly popular; Britain's entry into the European Economic Community in 1973 was against the wishes of a substantial proportion of the people, and our involvement is still widely deplored. In each case, a generation or more of those opposed to a great breach with the past have felt disregarded, and have remained resentful and unwilling to surrender their identity, so deeply do they feel defined by what others regard as mere contingencies.

In the longest run, however, even abrupt and momentous political and social changes may be accepted if they are not utterly contrary to man's nature. At the end of *Thoughts on French Affairs* (1791), Burke writes:

> If a great change is to be made in human affairs, the minds of men will be fitted to it; the general opinions and feelings will draw that way. Every fear, every hope will forward it; and then they who persist in opposing this mighty current in human affairs will appear rather to resist the decrees of Providence itself, than the mere designs of men. They will not be resolute and firm, but perverse and obstinate.

"That return of Burke upon himself has always seemed to me one of the finest things in English literature, or indeed in any literature," commented Matthew Arnold in "The Function of Criticism at the Present Time". For by conceding that what he dreads might well happen – as it did – Burke reaches out beyond his circumstances. He always spoke up for the capacity to recognize contradictory principles, and here he shows that he has the ability and the humility, for all his firmness and resolution, to see another possibility. He fears, as he wrote in a letter of November 29, 1792, that "the whole nation will change its character, if it has not changed it, as I strongly suspect it has, already". But he has no desire to be proved right. In a letter to the future Prime Minister George Canning, on March 1, 1797, he is noble enough to hope that his fears will prove unfounded: "No man wishes more than I do, that all my ideas should be found vain and frivolous upon experience."

The forms that Burke pleaded for may not endure, but his principles can find new applications. He did not win his epic battles, but he lives for other days. This flexibility makes him unlike the sloganizing French revolutionaries, unlike Marxists. But he is also unlike the brand of modern Conservative who intones the mantra of the market whatever the problem, without conceding that free markets can loosen the bonds of society. One important lesson from his life is that we should be vigilant about our principles, asking always whether they still apply, or whether other principles better meet the present case. Arnold's appreciation of Burke's return upon himself continues:

> That is what I call living by ideas: when one side of a question has long had your earnest support, when all your feelings are engaged, when you hear all round you no language but one, when your party talks this language like a steam-engine and can imagine no other, – still to be able to think, still to be irresistibly carried, if so it be, by the current of thought to the opposite side of the question and, like Balaam, to be unable to speak anything *but what the Lord has put in your mouth.*

The trouble with systems is that they seem to absolve us from this duty of staying alert, and this means we are liable to become caught up in the machine and mangled. Burke always opposed the mechanical application of ideas, and Arnold's image of a steam-engine banging away shows exactly the danger of an automatic politics. Cases must be judged on their merits. As Arnold says, "the great safeguard is never to let oneself become abstract, always to retain an intimate and lively consciousness of the truth of what one is saying, and, the moment this fails us, to be sure that something is wrong".

No political theory or principle is infallible, but there is a crucial distinction. Theory sets itself no limits, whereas principle is more modest. In his essay "Literary Principles as against Theory",

Christopher Ricks characterizes "the greatest of English critics", Dr Johnson:

> his greatness is not distinct from his sustained and rational opposition to philosophy and to theory. "The task of criticism" was, for Johnson, to "establish principles" (*Rambler*, No 92), and he everywhere made clear that his refusal to elaborate and concatenate the needed concepts beyond a certain point (a point reached early) was not a refusal to continue to think, but a decision to think thereafter about the application of the principles and not to elaborate principle into theory.
>
> (*Essays in Appreciation.*)

As with Johnson in the literary field, so with Burke in the political. In his *Letter to a Member of the National Assembly* (1791) he refuses to "obtrude any project of mine upon a nation [France] to whose circumstances I could not be sure it might be applicable":

> I must see with my own eyes, I must, in a manner, touch with my own hands, not only the fixed but the momentary circumstances, before I could venture to suggest any political project whatsoever. I must know the power and disposition to accept, to execute, to persevere. I must see all the aids, and all the obstacles. I must see the means of correcting the plan, where correctives would be wanted. I must see the things; I must see the men.

A writer said by many to be reckless in his denunciation of the revolution is here modest and cautious. Whilst standing by his principles, for he was never the advocate of raw expediency, he refuses to theorize. He speaks not of ideas but of "things" and "correctives". He is like a man with a pair of scales and weights of diminishing size but increasing delicacy. His prudent words are widely applicable – they exemplify principle – but could never be called a theory.

In January 1789, during the Regency crisis, when George III fell mad and there was much discussion of the theoretical extent of the emergency powers of his son, Burke wrote in a letter to William Windham, that whatever may be speculatively the case, any principle "can bear a practical superstructure of only a certain weight". Yet political theory since the 18th century has continued to search for a foundation that will bear an infinite load. Burke's objection applies as much to the systems of Marx, Mill, Lenin or Rawls as to those of Rousseau and Paine. And yet in another remarkable display of integrity, Burke refuses to condemn, any more than to praise, in the abstract; in the *Reflections* he writes: "I reprobate no form of government merely upon abstract principles. There may be situations in which the purely democratic form will become necessary."

Sir Joshua Reynolds, whose portrait of Burke is perhaps the truest, died in 1792, whereupon Burke wrote some notes about his friend, beginning: "He was a great generalizer, and was fond of reducing everything to one system, more perhaps than the variety of principles which operate as in the human mind and in every human work will properly endure." Burke's emphasis, as always, is on the variety of principles and the uncomfortable squeeze that is necessary to reduce them to one system. But as if not to be systematically opposed to systems, he immediately concedes the other side of the case: "But this disposition to abstractions, generalizing and classifications is the great glory of the human mind. . ." Despite his loathing of theories and generalizations exaggerated into untruths, he wrote elsewhere: "I do not put abstract ideas wholly out of any question, because I well know that under that name I should dismiss principles." It is this openness and continual searching for truth that helps to explain why, despite his many memorable sayings, it is difficult to reduce Burke's thought to a portable philosophy. So much is lost in translation; so much depends upon circumstances.

5

Putting the World to Rights

Burke condemned "the metaphysicians of our time" as "the most foolish of men". He realized that whereas scientific and mathematical ideas can often be examined by logical extrapolation, metaphysical ideas such as rights lapse into paradox and absurdity if taken too far. "The very habit of stating these extreme cases is not very laudable or safe," he wrote in the *Appeal to the Old Whigs*. The casuist's subtlety and extenuations cast all in doubt, and Burke condemns the adherents of the new "Frenchified Whiggism" (including his former friend Fox) for their recklessness, in a great letter of January 31, 1792, to his fellow MP for Malton, William Weddell: "They are sublime metaphysicians; and the horrible consequences produced by their speculations affect them not at all. They only ask whether the proposition be true? – whether it produces good or evil is no part of their concern."

In 1774, hoping for conciliation with America, he urged ministers not to press the "right" to tax to its disastrous conclusion: "I am not here going into the distinctions of rights, nor attempting to mark their boundaries. I do not enter into these metaphysical distinctions; I hate the very sound of them." He did not care to argue with theories of right and sovereignty, but urged that these would all be vain without the Americans' consent. He said that the colonists were enraged not by their subjection in principle to British rule – as long as this had been beneficial to them they had not questioned its legitimacy – but by the imposition of unprecedented taxes. It was this breach of the prescribed arrangement that called the whole relationship in question.

Two years later, with the Declaration of Independence of 1776, the Americans explicitly withdrew their consent, with the words "governments are instituted among men, deriving their just powers from the consent of the governed"; and within seven years, the wisdom of Burke's empirical imperial policy was proven. The Americans had broken away because Britain had pressed its "right" to tax them. "Oh! miserable and infatuated ministers!"

declared Burke in the Commons, on November 27, 1781, "miserable and undone country! not to know that right signifies nothing without might, that the claim without the power of enforcing it was nugatory and idle."

Many of the "rights" proclaimed today have the same hollow, metaphysical ring. Ignoring circumstances, they exist only in "the infinite void of the conjectural world". It is no use, for example, invoking rights as a rhetorical protection on behalf of those who are powerless in the face of persecution. The totem will not save them. Outsiders may feel more comfortable for having invoked the supposed rights of the oppressed, but as Burke wrote, "all virtue which is impracticable is spurious". Whatever our international resolutions may be, rights are anything but universal: their applicability is inevitably subject to local circumstances. The poor of Africa have no means even to claim much of what the abundance of the West guarantees to us before we ask. Abstract rights are to be mistrusted because they abstract the idea from the practice, and so consider separately things which are inseparable. "What is the use of discussing a man's abstract right to food or to medicine?" asks Burke. "The question is upon the method of procuring and administering them."

As the 18th-century optimists discovered, pompous protocols, charters and declarations easily become substitutes for actions. The United Nations outlaws genocide; the European Union issues a guideline that there should be no more than 76 parts per billion of ozone in the air; but these resolutions highlight the impotence of officialdom in the face of mass murder or pollution. Who is to vindicate these helpless rights? Declarations that might be useful as targets can be harmful when they are left to fulfil themselves. "Let compassion be shown in action, the more the better," wrote Burke of the poor, in his *Thoughts and Details on Scarcity* (1795). "Patience, labour, sobriety, frugality, and religion, should be recommended to them; all the rest is downright *fraud*."

The rights of people to be protected from having this or that wrong done to them have gradually led on to hypothetical rights to have this or that done *for* them. And the assertion or promise of such rights supposes the intervention of some agency. Usually it means empowering the state (or superstate), and so curtailing private liberties and discretion. But, "To provide for us in our necessities is not in the power of government. It would be a vain presumption in statesmen to think they can do it. The people maintain them, and not they the people. It is in the power of government to prevent much evil; it can do very little positive good in this, or perhaps in anything else." The Soviet Union attempted to prove Burke's view wrong – and was prepared to pay the price of freedom – yet eventually it collapsed, like a fixed exchange-rate attempting to defy the markets. No state can provide or guarantee life's necessities, which is why the call upon resources that is an asserted right to something is ultimately mistaken. It is an error to assume that because people need food, shelter, medical care, clothes and so on, sufficient supplies must exist and are being denied them out of malice or greed or maladministration. Some needs are not met because they cannot be. Needs cannot simply be transmuted into rights. The danger of declaring that "the pursuit of happiness" is among the "unalienable rights" of men is that men will elide this into a right to happiness, and will come to believe, unreasonably, that it is the state's business to ensure it. People have a biological need for sex and intimacy, but it would be an extraordinary government which promised these. To call these "rights" would be to oblige others to meet the need. In practice, not all such needs will be or can be met, and some might exact a price not worth paying.

The sort of confusion bred by our culture of "rights" and our over-extended welfare system was illustrated by a 15-year-old mother, interviewed on radio, who said plaintively: "I don't want anything that costs money, just a place to live and someone to love me." She was bewildered and felt she had been sold short. Hadn't society implicitly promised these things? It was, she thought, up to other people to house her – and presumably up to them, too, to find someone to love her. With the best will in the world, we have betrayed her.

Good intentions are often counterproductive. The idea of a "children's charter" laying down particular rights, for instance, pretends that children should have rights like everyone else. But children are not yet like everyone else: they are not fully formed or fully responsible. Rather than the autonomy of independent rights, they need the shelter of people to depend upon, who will restrain, discipline, guide and love them. Their capacities are still developing. Children are not equal to adults, though no less important. As a "passenger's charter" enshrines what the passenger can expect from public transport, and a "citizen's charter" enshrines what the citizen can expect from the state, so a "children's charter" would pretend to enshrine what a child can expect from its parents. But how can the state guarantee that these expectations will be fulfilled? It cannot, so the idea is an imposture.

A "children's charter" would grotesquely invite children to litigate against their parents, as though they could win back their childhood or be compensated for its loss, or as though the process would not destroy the family. But children do not have sufficient understanding of consequences to prosecute their parents, and to have lawyers latch onto them in order to bring such cases is a form of exploitation. So the analogy with adult charters and the usefulness of the idea both collapse.

The responsibility of parents should not be diminished, nor their authority weakened, by a charter. Discipline naturally begins within the family, which means relying upon the loving discrimination of parents. Except in highly unusual cases, parents should have the ultimate authority, and children should not be encouraged to appeal to formal documents. The politicization of childhood should be resisted. Family life must not be reduced to a contract.

The idea of such a charter also implies that the way children should be treated can be defined. Yet the call of children upon us is unlimited. They deserve much more than could be written into a charter of rights, yet no charter could guarantee even what it specified. It would be an exercise in vanity among adults. Children need their parents, yet it is impossible to legislate that no young child's parents shall ever die. Nor can the love that children need be expressed as a right. To pretend that it can is to lose sight of an instinctive relationship, well expressed by Stewart Deuchar and Barbara Hug as "the wonderful arrangement whereby each generation starts deeply indebted to the previous one – for life itself, if nothing else – and pays off this debt to the next" (*The Salisbury Review*, December 1995). Instincts will always be stronger than rights.

The idea of a "children's charter" is instructive, too, about the glib reply frequently tendered when the excess of rights is mentioned: that rights are well and good so long as they are balanced by duties. Does this mean that we must have a Universal Declaration of Human Duties? Is it supposed that these too can be quantified, explicated and policed? Are parents' duties to their children to be expressed in this way? Does a child have rights only so long as it is dutiful? Has an infant rights only while it behaves? No: forces more elemental than the law are at work here, and we belittle ourselves if we suppose that it alone can comprehend them.

The rights of man were supposed to herald a new age of freedom and happiness. Instead, the mentality they encourage, of writing down one's hopes and blaming others if they are disappointed, is among the most ingrained of our present discontents.

Burke did occasionally speak of natural rights and natural law, but his conception of them developed in the course of his career, and exactly what he thought has been the subject of controversy. The term "natural rights" conflates two ideas: that of rights above the realm of human law, and that of rights which existed before the beginning of society. Burke endorsed the first idea, but thought the working of these arcane rights could not be fully mastered or provided for by man. The laws of nature, in ethics as in physics, are not simple and cannot be understood in isolation from one another. About the historical idea of natural rights, Burke was ambivalent, because the situation was hypothetical. He did not believe that there was anything natural about man outside society: he wanted men to go on living in the artificial state of civilization which is the sophisticated expression of man's true nature. His *Vindication of Natural Society*, after all, was satirical. In the words of Harvey Mansfield, "the *real* rights of men are to be found in a complicated social structure, not in a pre-civil state of nature".

In Burke's *Tract Relative to the Laws Against Popery in Ireland*, which he drafted around 1761 but did not publish, he wrote:

> Everybody is satisfied that a conservation and secure enjoyment of our natural rights is the great and ultimate purpose of civil society; and that therefore all forms whatsoever of government are only good as they are subservient to that purpose, to which they are entirely subordinate.

He argues that human laws are only declaratory, and that injustice does not become justice by a change in the law. However, he did not believe that the eternal laws or original justice or natural rights could be definitively codified. Written laws must always arise from particular traditions and circumstances. The divine will could not be brought once and for all within the human compass. "Nothing universal can be rationally affirmed on any moral, or political subject," he stated. But increasingly, men were attempting to do just that, so increasingly the need was not to convince people of the existence of these original rights, but to warn against misapplications or mistaken extensions of them.

By 1790, Burke was pouring scorn upon grand universal claims:

> Abstract principles were what his clumsy apprehension could not grasp; he must have a principle embodied in some manner or other, and the conduct held upon it ascertained, before he could pretend to judge of its propriety and advantage in practice. But of all abstract principles, abstract principles of natural right – which the dissenters rested on, as their stronghold – were the most idle, because the most useless and the most dangerous to resort to. They superseded society, and broke asunder all those bonds which had formed the happiness of mankind for ages. He would venture to say that if they were to go back abstractedly to original rights, there would be an end of all society. Abstract principles of natural right had been long since given up for the advantage of having, what was much better, society, which substituted wisdom and justice in the room of original right. It annihilated all those natural rights, and drew to its mass all the component parts of which those rights were made up. It took in all the virtue of the virtuous, all the wisdom of the wise.
>
> (*Parliamentary History*, XXVIII, 434.)

Since Burke was renowned for his extraordinary knowledge of men and ideas, the modest irony about his "clumsy apprehension" vividly makes the point that the metaphysical speculators were grasping at air. What is beyond his prehensile powers was unlikely to be within theirs. He does not say that there are no natural rights, but his metaphor suggests that their embodiment is crucial.

Burke knows he cannot take hold of an abstraction, but once it is embodied in characters and circumstances and actions, he can and will pass judgment. Various forms of oppression he judges to be breaches of natural rights. Genocide does not need to be defined by international commission before it is wrong. In impeaching Warren Hastings for his murderous regime in India, Burke spoke of his offences as "crimes not against morals, but against those eternal laws of justice which you [the House of Lords] are assembled here to assert. Not in formal and technical language but in real and absolute effect they are high crimes and misdemeanours." Against the interests of his countrymen and many fellow MPs, Burke upheld the welfare of strangers whom he had never met and who could never thank him.

Of the importance of natural rights before the development of society, Burke was increasingly sceptical, for in the process of civilization these were superseded by more important civil and social rights. Natural rights in this sense were trivial, because men live, of necessity and by their wish, in societies. "In a state of *rude* nature", he writes in his *Appeal to the Old Whigs*,

> there is no such thing as a people. A number of men in themselves have no collective capacity. The idea of a people is the idea of a corporation. It is wholly artificial; and made like all other legal fictions by common agreement. What the particular nature of that agreement was, is collected from the form into which the particular society has been cast. Any other is not *their* covenant. When men, therefore, break up the original compact or agreement which gives its corporate form and capacity to a state, they are no longer a people. . . With them all is to begin again.

In pooling their rights to freedom, men were entitled to be governed by consent, within the particular rules that had been developed.

In considering natural rights, then, Burke rejects the modern, transcendental sense. "As to abstract rights of all kinds, he thought they were incorporeal, and unfit for the body. They might be discussed in some other state; but they were totally unfit for this life. . ." (*Parliamentary History*, XXIX, 1388). The kind of rights he wished to uphold in practice were not *a priori* rights, but rights sanctioned by precedent, history, custom. When he asserts that his life's effort has been "to support with unrelaxing vigilance every right, every privilege, every franchise . . . under the protection of the British Crown", he is adverting not to universal but to particular, prescribed and established rights, "belonging to the people of this kingdom without any reference whatever to any other more general or prior right". The grouping of these with privileges and franchises is deliberate: these rights are a kind of private property – belongings – not speculative entitlements. Burke looks not for their origins, but to their present and active existence, and to their continuance. If a village has a right of way across a field, the people own their traditional access as surely as the farmer owns the field – and Burke would uphold both properties. But a right of way across another field can no more be conjured up by assertion than the ownership of a neighbour's house can simply be arrogated. Which is why Burke considered the new revolutionary dogma as an attempt to vindicate theft: "a contempt of *all* prescriptive titles, thence to the pillage of *all* property, and thence to universal desolation". In France, new rights went hand in hand with the destruction of old titles of ownership.

In the fog of hypothetical "rights", moral obligations become lost. The certain fact of a wrong is stronger, more rooted in the personal sense of morality, in our nature and second nature, than the abstraction of a "right". Scepticism about the terminology has been voiced by Noel Malcolm: "We might describe . . . freedom from arbitrary arrest and freedom from torture as things which we have a strong moral duty to respect. Having said that, haven't we said all we need to? What extra element of the argument is added by invoking the magic word 'rights'?" (*The Sunday Telegraph*, February 6, 1994).

Campaigners for rights treat them as sovereign, forgetting that they should be weighed and balanced. Rights may be based on useful principles, but then as Burke said, a principle will bear only so great a practical superstructure. The language of rights adopts a pseudo-philosophical severity when what is needed is a humane leniency. This makes it a ready disguise for insupportable claims. The "right to life" and the "right to choose" abortion are both principles, with claims to our respect (although claiming as a "right" what may be a necessary wrong is straining the language). Yet occasions differ, and to elevate either of these "rights" to the status of an absolute is to deny that the other could ever apply; to elevate *both* to this status excites vexatious questions and shows the inflexibility of theory as against principle. For "rights" have a tendency to be involved in head-on collisions, as the Chief Rabbi, Jonathan Sacks, has written:

> Does an author have the right to freedom of expression, or do religious groups have the right to protection against blasphemy? Do parents have the right to go their separate ways, or do children have the right to parental support? These questions generate fierce, even violent, controversy. But they cannot be answered in the terms in which they are asked. If we want to settle a conflict of rights, we must find some larger principle than rights.
>
> (*The Times*, May 31, 1994.)

These are among the most pressing political and social questions of our time, and the language of rights woefully misdescribes them and confuses us. Faced with claims such as the "right" to block the streets by demonstrating (now an intransitive verb), or the "right" of sado-masochists to inflict actual bodily harm upon each other, we should remember Burke's caution in the *Reflections*: "Men have no right to what is not reasonable." Unreasonable rights are spurious.

A (self-anointed) artist with a scheme to carve a white horse on a Wiltshire hillside is opposed by local people who like the landscape as it is; but he asserts that "as an artist" (and judge in his own case) he has a right to choose his site. The local people counter that they have a right to enjoy the hillside undisturbed. This escalating, abstract language cannot head off the collision between their wishes; nor does it suggest whose wishes should take priority. The terminology of entitlement makes for arrogance and inflexibility where Burke would have sought concessions, compromises and consensus – because "Magnanimity in politics is not seldom the truest wisdom."

Arguments from "rights" have no sense of proportion. Of the British constitution, Burke wrote, "take which of the principles you please – you will find its operation checked and stopped at a certain point". But the proclaimers of rights suppose them to be, like theory, not subject to circumscription. On the contrary, they *must* be unchecked. Those who deal in "universals and essences", Burke wrote, "see no difference between more and less". Essences are not matters of degree, and their proponents cannot cope with practical questions of priority. This leads to an absurd, unworldly outlook. The head of an environmental pressure group, asked to imagine that he had a budget of £1 billion, was unable to set out the spending priorities from his list of demands, because, he said, they simply must all be met in full. This sort of thinking is unable to compromise with reality and the art of the possible.

Rights cannot be unlimited, because all rights can be abused. Taken too far, they rebound upon us, as for instance when freedom of expression turns to gruesome and inciting pornography. Burke observed in 1775 that the exercise of certain rights in certain circumstances can be "the most odious of all wrongs, and the most vexatious of all injustice". The historian Edward Gibbon, much influenced by his reading of Burke's *Reflections*, wrote in similar terms to his friend Lord Sheffield: "You will be driven from one step to another, from principles just in theory to consequences most pernicious in practice" (May 30, 1792). This is exactly what has happened since then in many fields, and the exercise of rights to the utmost – each one clearing the way for a new claim – is again far less conciliatory than Burke's conception.

The advantage of Burke's prescriptive rights is that they base their appeal on the *status quo*, rather than justifying change by example, by analogy and by extension. The danger can be seen in the matter of building in restricted areas. For one reason or another, a planning committee makes a generous exception to a building ban and allows a new house. But once the new house has a *de facto* existence, it ceases to be a tolerated exception. The owners do not feel under sufferance, but in possession of their rights, and very soon their status is the same as that of earlier residents. They have an equal claim to consideration when they want to build another bathroom, or a garage. The planners' concession – this far and no farther – is swept away. A new building line becomes established, and the exception becomes a precedent for a further house, next door. Acceding to one claim generates another. Burke, however, resists the underlying fallacy that because one person is entitled to something, everyone else is too. In his thinking, people must be allowed to hold what they have, but have no abstract right to what they desire or to what others may possess.

"They have 'the rights of men'," wrote Burke sarcastically in the *Reflections*. "Against these there can be no prescription; against these no agreement is binding: these admit no temperament, and no compromise: anything withheld from their full demand is so much of fraud and injustice." The language of "the rights of man" imagines them as unbounded entitlements inherent in the fact of our having been born, and concedes no moderating forces. But we arrived in a world of limited resources, and so our rights – our claims upon the world – must be circumscribed.

It may be useful to think of most "rights" as limited prerogatives or privileges, like parking permits. My permit entitles me to park on my street. But the entitlement is not absolute: there comes a day when there are no spaces. This may be because someone without a permit has parked – an infringement – or it may be because my neighbour, who does have a permit, has parked with his caravan. Our rights, which we both took to be clear, are in conflict. Even in this case, where there is an agreed legal contract – a permit to park – no right can be guaranteed: I have *permission* to park, but the means may not exist for me to exercise it. Furthermore, the houses in the street are being divided into flats, and more and more people reasonably expect to be granted permits. So their rights are diminishing mine. And this is just what is happening as the world becomes more crowded with people and their claims. Some of what I propound as my rights diminish the liberties of others; the more people propound them, the more rights are likely to be degraded. Few can have imagined in 1915, when cars were rare, that the "right" to drive would become controversial. But as everybody takes to the road, we find ourselves in a jam. It becomes intolerable, a source of conflict. Then the "right" to clean air is counterclaimed: your freedom to drive is reducing my ability to breathe. A kind of inflation is at work. The more rights are promulgated, the more they are devalued.

These problems are worst in cities. The owners of an isolated farm in Wales are unlikely to cause offence by holding a noisy party. They would not be so free in Highgate. As Burke pragmatically put it, "the *situations* in which men relatively stand produce the rules and principles of [their] responsibility". Rights, then, are relative to other considerations; we do better not to translate our conflicts into a realm beyond the actual and practical.

To some degree we can increase and extend human blessings; the world can make itself richer, can distribute its food better. But it cannot conjure up new habitable territories, so the "right" to a place to live, for instance, cannot be absolute. (How big is a "place"?) Nor can we guarantee the "right" of every patient to a kidney transplant. Even if money were infinite, some medical resources would be limited. Yet the temptation to reinforce every social and political demand – legitimate or otherwise – with the word "rights" has proved irresistible. As with bogus demands for public spending, it is easier for politicians to capitulate to bogus rights than to explain why they should not or cannot be countenanced, why the "right" does not apply or does not extend so far. Consequently, an ever-expanding realm of entitlements has led to an ever-expanding public expenditure. Thomas Paine was a poor prophet when he wrote in *The Rights of Man* that revolutions "have for their object, a change in the moral condition of governments, and with this change the burden of public taxes will lessen". On the contrary, since the revolutionary moral change at the end of the 18th century, the burden of the state has weighed heavier and heavier. Neither philosophically nor fiscally can this growth be supported, and it will at last have to be curtailed.

On the French revolutionary ideas, Burke wrote in his *Appeal to the Old Whigs*: "The pretended *rights of man*, which have made this havoc, cannot be the rights of the people. For to be a people, and to have these rights, are things incompatible. The one supposes the presence, the other the absence of a state of civil society." He argued that no civil or political right could ever be indefeasible. However, the utopian simplicities of "that Jacobin incendiary" Thomas Paine are still current – for such promises are more immediately seductive than Burke's sophisticated compounds. The rights of the individual have been pressed ever more insistently, they crowd in upon us, to the detriment of society. Ironically, nominally "universal" rights have not bound people together, but have made them think ever more of themselves as individuals and groups apart from, and wronged by, society.

The rights that have been asserted are now legion, occasionally contradictory, and often quite impossible to secure. Some express little more than a wish that someone else should provide the desirable things in life and compensate for its hardships. Usually the someone else is the impersonalized state, because claims upon it appear to be less of an imposition than those upon other individuals. But this is like the mistaken idea that insurance fraud is a "victimless" crime. Incrementally, we all pay the price of selfish claims.

The poet George Crabbe (to whom Burke was a generous

patron in a time of abject need) was alert to such impostures in "The Parish Register" (1807):

> 'Twas his, at cards each Novice to trepan,
> And call the Wants of Rogues the Rights of Man.

Crabbe saw how, by sleight of hand, matters of moral importance are confounded with trivial grievances and wishful thinking (and not always for honourable purposes). The United Nations Declaration of Human Rights, for instance, includes the "right" to paid holidays: bad rights mock the good.

After earnest centuries of trying, such demands remain resistant to codification. The law is intrinsically less good at providing positive benefits than at proscribing wrongs or obtaining redress ("the prevention of evils is the great object of all good regulation," said Burke). Ross Clark has written:

> It is moral to treat your fellow man as you would wish to be treated yourself; that you should not kill him unless he is threatening your life. It is also moral not to allow your fellow man to starve if you can feed him. A code of human morality existed in a recognizable form across most religions long before the language of rights was invented by Thomas Paine, Thomas Jefferson and the United Nations. But to repackage morality in a passive form and say that all men have a right to eat is unnecessary and misleading.
>
> (*The Sunday Telegraph*, March 12, 1995.)

Britain, unlike other countries, has preferred not to try to establish what positive rights and duties the people have. Our principal rights are our freedoms. In other countries, which a few malcontents would have Britain emulate, the long search for definitive rights has not yet produced agreement about what they might be. Each "progressive" generation has new standards, and looks at what it has inherited not with gratitude, but as a cause for dissatisfaction. There is always something that government does not supply or underwrite, and that failing can be described to the credulous as disgraceful. Why, for instance, does the government not "compensate" the relatives of victims of this or that kind of accident or medical error or trauma? Why does it not reward Olympic medallists in cash? Or subsidize the film industry? But why should it?

Burke saw that the state – or a political party – should not bribe the people with promises. For if it cannot keep them (as in the case of bogus rights) it breaches the public trust; and if it does keep them it must shortly offer further promises as fresh bribes. Late in his career, he wrote that it is becoming to consider and respect the rights of others, while expressing our own claims only as requests:

> If the subject thinks so highly and reverently of the sovereign authority as not to claim anything of right, so that it may seem to be independent of the power and free choice of its government; and if the sovereign, on his part, considers the advantages of the subjects as their right, and all their reasonable wishes as so many claims; in the fortunate conjunction of these mutual dispositions are laid the foundations of a happy and prosperous commonwealth.
>
> (*A Letter to Sir Hercules Langrishe*, 1792.)

That politics should be other than a clash of demands between selfish interests now looks a lot to ask or even to imagine. But we have tried the other way. A return to Burke's ideas of equity and consent, in place of our unrealistic ideas of equality and rights, might help to rescue us from strangulating and mistrustful legalism. It might also restore gratitude to public life. For while people are usually grateful for and protective of what they see as their privileges, many are oblivious to the cost and effort expended upon providing what they consider to be theirs by right. Established democracies generally have lower turnouts at elections than new ones, where the people are thankful for the opportunity to vote. Similarly, now that education is not only a right but is compulsory up to the age of 16, many children are contemptuous of opportunities and advantages that their forebears would have embraced with appreciation and a sense of obligation. If we believe that we have an inalienable entitlement to something, and that no one can take it away, we may fail to be properly grateful for it. People who would have felt gratitude for charitable alms, for instance, may not for state benefits. Extending our entitlements can work to annul some of the sentiments which bind us together, and which make both giving and receiving morally satisfactory.

In the most famous passage he ever wrote, in *Reflections on the Revolution in France*, Burke laments: "But the age of chivalry is gone. – That of sophisters, economists, and calculators, has succeeded; and the glory of Europe is extinguished for ever." His immediate subject is the shocking treatment of the Queen of France,

Marie Antoinette, but his larger point is about a code of courtesy and mutual respect between the sexes, between ranks, between rulers and ruled, which – in his idealized picture – made society harmonious. He saw elaborate emotional bonds being broken, as old affections gave way to a new disaffection.

> But now all is to be changed. All the pleasing illusions, which made power gentle, and obedience liberal, which harmonized the different shades of life, and which, by a bland assimilation, incorporated into politics the sentiments which beautify and soften private society, are to be dissolved by this new conquering empire of light and reason.

Philip Francis, Burke's colleague in impeachment of Hastings, attacked these pages when they were still in proof as "pure foppery"; Paine regarded chivalry as a "farce", and today the word may sound like archaic posturing. But Burke was writing about much more than an affected gallantry. His term "chivalry" comprehended a whole system of values, a whole dimension of life, that was then in danger and now seems at its last gasp. He grants at once that the conventions and susceptibilities of chivalry, of deferring to the needs and wishes of others, were "illusions" – artificially constructed modes of behaviour; but unlike the new construction of rights, which put the self first, the old ways had helped to extend into the public realm something of the generosity and grace of private life. As we are discovering, living without such codes is hellish.

In a letter, Burke wishes that people should be "modest and placable". Sadly, we have lost or are losing even the word, while "implacable" marches on. But *to make power gentle and obedience liberal*: how much nobler that aim is than any espoused in our disenchanted, illusionless world.

6

Democracy and Consent

To examine Burke's use of words is to discover how much values have changed. To him, for instance, "visionary" always means illusory or delusive, never blessed with grand ideas or foresight. "Innovation" – an idol of our century – was for him an abominable deviation (and in Shakespeare it is always associated with insurrection and treachery). "Original" is now the most routine term of praise, but that laudatory sense is not recorded in Dr Johnson's *Dictionary* of 1755. On the other hand, in painting and literary composition – for Reynolds and Johnson – "imitation" was an important and instructive discipline.

Far more than our 18th-century forebears, we value novelty and individuality. And yet more than they, we live by the rule of the mass. "Democracy", which for Burke meant the threat of mob rule, is the scarcely challenged faith of our times. Our culture now uses the shibboleth "democratic" loosely, to mean politically healthy and fair. No proposal for change is made without the protective label "democratic" being tied to it, and many minds seem unable to hold any other idea or principle alongside this one. A universal franchise is considered the only basis of political legitimacy, regardless of circumstance or history. Its introduction is required without regard to the consequences, even where it will enable one tribal or racial group to use weight of numbers to oppress another. In places with mixed affiliations, such as Northern Ireland or Africa or the former Yugoslavia, democracy can become a pretext for the persecution of minorities.

The prejudice in favour of "democracy" (for the case is no longer argued) is so strong that any restraint upon the people's will is thoughtlessly presumed to be *a priori* wrong, and so emotive is the word that to question its omnicompetence is considered a tasteless betrayal of freedom. Anything that can be called "undemocratic" is beyond the pale. "Is it then a truth so universally acknowledged, that a pure democracy is the only tolerable form into which human society can be thrown, that a man is not permitted to hesitate about its merits without the suspicion of being a friend to tyranny, that is, of being a foe to mankind?" Burke's question was a rhetorical one expecting the answer "no"; but today it is only in circles of sophisticated and academic political discussion that the failings of democracy are acknowledged, and such a considered case is hardly ever put before, say, the mighty television audience.

Democracy is an honourable and venerable principle, but principles admit the possibility of counter-principles, which may apply in other ways or other circumstances, and it is these that are disregarded by democratic zealots. Justice is a principle, but it does not exclude mercy; indeed Burke writes that "Mercy is not a thing opposed to justice. It is an essential part of it. . ." Similarly, the principle of democracy should not exclude the principles of restraint and discipline which are essential parts of it. Democracy needs to respect kinds of experience and wisdom which may never put themselves forward for election or which might never appeal to a mass electorate: these too are necessary if it is to work well. Unfortunately, however, democracy has been elevated into a utilitarian test, with the greatest number being treated as the greatest good – or at least as irresistible. At first this sounds attractive, but as the 19th-century Utilitarians found, such a mechanism needs modification if it is not to result in oppression – or even elimination – of awkward minorities. "Of this I am certain," wrote Burke in the *Reflections*, "that in a democracy, the majority of citizens is capable of exercising the most cruel oppressions upon the minority".

Dean Inge offered a caution: "Democracy is only an experiment in government, and it has the obvious disadvantage of merely counting votes instead of weighing them." However, what to Inge and Burke was a dubious hypothesis is now supposed a theorem, a proven rule, as though in a controlled experiment it had been shown to be the best solution to political dissatisfactions. Yet somehow the dissatisfactions persist. Ways to implement democracy are debated, but in popular opinion (which counts only itself), the democratic ideal is sufficient and above scrutiny. There is little public acknowledgment of the need for countervailing forces. We are proud to have widened the franchise, but we do not see that we have narrowed the basis of politics. Yet just as we hate the threat of a one-party state, we should hate the threat of a one-principle state. Burke would never have accepted public opinion as the sole standard of truth. There is more to government than a show of hands.

The democratic principle is based upon inclusive representation. If the affairs of the nation are decided by elected politicians, all adults have had a chance, indirectly, to influence events. But a political system should aim to make decisions that are just to everyone (not only the loudest or largest group), and which are well-informed and capable of enduring. This is a more difficult matter. Democracy aims to be an institutionalized compromise, a form of averaging out. The hope is that extreme measures are unlikely to find favour with a majority. This assumes that while one person may make a mistake, the mass is less easily deluded. But the assumption is unsafe, for mobs are readily swayed, and more by emotion than argument. Acting as a body is the attractive power of crowds, and a mass is not always moderate. Once a fashion or trend begins, or an opinion becomes popular, the bulk of people tend to move the same way, to behave as others suggest, to do what they are told or incited to do. It is a mistake to suppose that people's errors will cancel one another out, for in practice people come under the same misleading influences simultaneously – gaining their impressions, say, from one erroneous documentary or advertisement – and so are likely all to make the same mistake at once. Then the aggregation is overwhelming. In a democracy, ten people acting for one weak or fallacious reason, or for none at all, will always outweigh one person with ten strong and cogent arguments for doing something else.

In our populist democracy, more people than ever before take a casual interest in politics, as they do in other spectator sports, and what is at stake is simplified for them. The mass media are skilled at finding the essential elements of an issue. But the preference for the strong and straightforward is often taken to the point of distortion, and disagreements are often reduced to a clash of personalities. What is "plain and simple must", in Burke's words, "be easily understood by those who would be brought with great difficulty to comprehend the intricate detail". So immediately attractive notions are likely to triumph over complex or compound considerations. "The little catechism of the rights of men is soon learned," writes Burke – but a recognition of its consequences takes much longer.

People are impatient. Paine's politics will always have more adherents than Burke's, just as Newton's physics is always going to be more widely understood than Einstein's; but at least scientists are not governed by the public's opinion of who was right. Technical knowledge advances when pioneers investigate what everyone else takes for granted: that the world is flat, or that heavier-than-air machines cannot fly. On the other hand, politics as presently understood can less and less afford to ignore what the popular press urges the mass to believe. Year by year, political parties, like other aspects of public life, defer a little more to the taste and opinions that have been foisted upon the majority. Unfortunately, the pursuit of ratings alone is as ruinous to good government as to good television.

In newspapers and on television, polling is increasing. What other people think – "our survey said" – is now news, and is in danger of being taken for truth, or of trumping the facts, with which it is frequently at odds. For as well as being self-important, opinion polling is self-fulfilling. When people are polled about whether there should be a poll or referendum about this or that, the act of asking them makes it seem that their opinion is what matters, so they say yes. This is good news for the polling companies (more work), but it may not be good for the procedures of government, for it encourages the idea that a democratic vote applies to everything. Polling promotes democracy, where it is appropriate and where it is not. It is also iconoclastic. It treats nothing as settled. Everything becomes a possible cause of dissent and dispute, because the pollster can encourage people to question anything.

Opinion polls are predicated upon the importance of popular opinion, and yet they demonstrate how febrile and uncertain the unmediated wishes of the public usually are. People lack information about their options, and the likely consequences, and cannot express their choices coherently. Enormous power is assumed by the framer of the questions. During discussions in the summer of 1996 about a referendum on Britain's involvement in the European Union, opinion polls tried to gauge popular feeling. But the populace didn't know what it felt. Of those expressing a view, 43 per cent favoured "coming out of Europe", but only 19 per cent favoured "a complete British withdrawal", while 34 per cent thought British membership a bad thing. Some 60 per cent opposed further transfer of powers to the Europe, and yet there were majorities for a common legal system and for common taxation (because three out of four people did not realise that Britain's taxes were the lowest in the EU). This is more muddled even than Conservative Party policy in the 1990s, and certainly could not be a basis for government. The people must be able to vote for this party or that, but they are incompetent to determine the details of policy or to adjudicate on such specialized issues as the merits of a single European currency. Nor should politicians pass on the responsibility – or blame – to the citizens, who are largely uninterested, uninformed and otherwise occupied. To make the pollster the polestar is destructive, because opinion is so fickle.

Yet polls are pointing the way towards government by national mass-meeting, with the people making every decision and their own sovereign mistakes. Nothing – no mediators, no moderators, no interpreters – need come between the semi-coherent will of the majority and the enacting of edicts, given the necessary technology. But what technology enables, it might also determine, for the pressure from lobby groups, advertizing and big business, as they attempt to influence popular votes, would become all-pervasive. Far from being passive, the media would determine outcomes, first telling people what to think and then polling them.

Soon, interactive television could produce a true tabloid democracy, in which the will of the people would be law. The political class could abdicate its responsibilities, extinguishing – in the words of the *Reflections* – "all moral principle, all sense of dignity, all use of judgment, and all consistency of character". There would be no great and good, no royal commissions, no think-tanks, no ministerial advisers on education or health or defence. We would need neither representatives nor even delegates, for an electronic running referendum much more accurate and comprehensive than opinion polls will shortly be possible. Already, *The Sun* has pioneered a version of this, by mischievously asking its readers to phone in to vote on such issues as whether the Prince of Wales should ever become king. Thousands of readers take this sufficiently seriously to register their yea or nay – as though public opinion could constitutionally affect his prescriptive birthright. (Fortunately, the monarch holds the crown, to paraphrase the *Reflections*, in contempt of the readers of *The Sun*, who have not a single vote for a king amongst them. The monarch does not owe the crown to the choice of the people, though holding it in concurrence with their wishes. The newspaper and the pollsters make the same categorical error as the Revolution Society, which Burke denounced for proclaiming that the only principle on which a king could be lawfully recognized was the choice of the people.)

In future, democracy-on-the-box could decide not only the best Song for Europe or the goal of the season, but which tragic, photogenic child was to be the spending priority of the health service, regardless of the doctors' prognosis. And the peanut-crunching crowd could press its buttons now to find the defendant innocent or guilty, and again to decide whether the guilty should be hanged and whether the hanging should be televised. It is not only politicians with jobs to protect who can see that the diktat of the mass expressed in this way would be immoderate, capricious and ignorant beyond any government. "For this reason no legislator, at any period of the world, has willingly placed the seat of active power in the hands of the multitude: Because there it admits of no control, no regulation, no steady direction whatsoever," wrote Burke in his *Appeal to the Old Whigs*. "The people are the natural control on authority; but to exercise and to control together is contradictory and impossible."

If politicians were to cease to exercise authority, on a democratic theory, the responsibility would not pass to the people, for an unled herd cannot be responsible. Responsibility would evaporate. As in the French Revolution events would occur apparently at random, without cause, consequence or understanding. The all-powerful crowd would not learn from experience, and the situation would be extremely unstable.

Just as a free market takes little account of, say, long-term environmental problems, so an aggregate of mass opinion will scarcely consider some large moral questions. In June 1784, as he was preparing to impeach Warren Hastings, Burke wrote in a letter to William Baker that it was clear that "all the tyranny, robbery and destruction of mankind" practised by the East India Company was "popular and pleasing in this country" so long as it brought wealth, and that therefore the complacency of the majority must be challenged by those possessed of a conscience and the facts. Many enterprises of state – such as conquering inflation – require a resolve and expertise which is hard enough to find among philosophers and statesmen, and which is not to be found at all in the minute-to-minute judgment of popular opinion. Burke argues, for instance, that the power of declaring war must reside in the steady hands of the monarchy,

> to secure us against popular rashness in plunging into wars, and against the effects of popular dismay, disgust or lassitude in getting out of them as imprudently as we might first engage in them. To have no other measure in judging of those great objects than our momentary opinions and desires, is to throw us back upon that very democracy which, in this part, our constitution was formed to avoid.
>
> (*Letters on a Regicide Peace*, 1796.)

The crucial antithesis here is between prudence and rashness. Promoting the one and resisting the other becomes more difficult all the time, as communications improve and reactions are expected ever more immediately. Yet as we contemplate the chaos of an electronic ultra-democracy, it becomes obvious that the will of the people must, as Burke knew, be mitigated.

Burke thought it the duty of MPs to be pillars of the state – not weathercocks of no use "but to indicate the shiftings of every popular gale". Policy ought to take into account factors other than the popular clamour. These should include tradition and experience, strategic thinking, intellectual coherence, budgetary necessity, ethics, and even aesthetic values. The ground for resistance to government by direct instruction from the populace must be that Parliament as a body has experience, a trained judgment and access to specialized knowledge (perhaps more evident in the Lords than the Commons), and that it has a duty to guide as well as to be guided by the people. "When it appears evident to our governors that our desires and our interests are at variance, they ought not to gratify the former at the expense of the latter." Or as Christopher Ricks has recently put it, "people's wishes may be insufficiently thought out, and we may have a duty not to collaborate with ill-judged ones" (*Bostonia*, Winter 1994–95).

Burke had the courage to see this principle through. In 1780, he told his Bristol constituents that he had not been bound by their assessment of the political questions concerning trade and America: "I did not obey your instructions. No. I conformed to the instructions of truth and nature, and maintained your interest, against your opinions, with a constancy that became me." But Burke was not re-elected for Bristol, and if even he could not persuade the then small number of relatively educated voters of the justice of his actions, there is a strong case against allowing the universal franchise always to decide whose counsel shall prevail.

Already, however, democracy is a television contest: a game increasingly determined by the rules and rulers of the media. Politicians may have different policies, but they must all appeal in the same way: telegenically. With the occasional exception of those with the deepest convictions, they risk becoming, in Burke's phrase, "flatterers instead of legislators; the instruments not the guides of the people" – and flattery "is the reverse of instruction". This outcome is undesirable and unacceptable to both sides: for legislators wish to exercise freedom of conscience, and the people generally wish to delegate to politicians the day-to-day business of governing, so that they are free to go about their own concerns. Instead, the people now find themselves unwilling to trust their politicians yet unable to regulate them either.

So why is democracy prized so highly and so automatically? Because the term is loosely used as the opposite of tyranny. It is a shorthand for respecting the wishes, welfare and liberty of all, as opposed to a sectarian rule or dictatorship. In 1947, Churchill famously said in the Commons: "No one pretends that democracy is perfect or all-wise. Indeed, it has been said that democracy is the worst form of government except all those other forms that have been tried from time to time." But he was not contrasting government by direct popular vote with "all those other forms" (which would have included that known and revered by Burke); he was contrasting tolerant, open government with the systems that he and his country had fought against so recently. In this sense, democracy is entirely laudable.

Burke too was a champion of the freedom of the people to be governed by consent, and of government on behalf of the people as a whole. But he would have wished to scrutinize the term "democracy" rigorously. For far from believing that democracy was the simple antithesis of tyranny, he knew that it could become a tyranny. He did not believe that the people, by head count, should run their own affairs directly (any more than we believe that lay parties going to law should generally represent themselves without professional advice in court). The simplistic slogan that "in every country the people is the legitimate sovereign" he rejects. "This confounds, in a manner equally mischievous and stupid, the origin of a government from the people with its continuance in their hands." And in an age more trusting than ours, he suggests that for their own sake, those in whom reason is weak should be excluded from the franchise. But in the context, his *Letter to Sir Hercules Langrishe*, Burke is arguing that "the most poor, illiterate and uninformed creatures upon earth" are the best judges of "a practical oppression", and that their distress must never be ignored, though they themselves may not understand "the *real cause*, or the *appropriate remedy*". The ignorant ought to be looked after by the better educated, the weak by the strong – and the educated and the strong have a duty of protection. His argument, as he had written the previous year in his *Appeal from the New to the Old Whigs* was "against literal government by the people, not against government controlled by the people".

Although he is renowned for saying that governors have a higher duty than obedience to the greatest number – which is to do their best by all citizens and for the general advantage – he wanted people and Parliament to be in harmony, and felt that a Parliament which did not enjoy the confidence and sympathy of the people was an imposition. "Let the Commons in Parliament assembled be one and the same thing with the commons at large", he proclaims; and again, "The virtue, spirit, and essence of a House of Commons consists in its being the express image of the feelings of the nation. It was not instituted to be a control *upon* the people. . . It was designed as a control *for* the people." This is not the voice of a repressive autocrat.

Democracy aims to be inclusive, but Burke's understanding is much more so – because it includes factors that democracy overlooks. His conception of inclusive government is also much more subtle. The danger, as he perceived – and as we see from the behaviour of elected governments – is that once voted in by all the people, democratic politicians tend to believe that they have a mandate to represent not the whole people, but much narrower interests. They become cliquish and are liable to be as despotic as absolute monarchs.

Any unmixed form of government has fewer ways of involving and engaging the people than a plural form. Pure monarchy and pure democracy have much in common, and neither extreme is desirable. Who can say what powers a democratic mandate cannot extend to? The people could vote in the death penalty for terrorists. Or for the elderly, or the ugly. Dictators, after all, have been brought to power by popular election.

Burke thought that pure democracies would fail for lack of counterbalances, being "wanting in caution, steadiness and system in their conduct on the most important occasions". So he would be disappointed to find that for all the current dissatisfaction with our politics, the principal proposals for constitutional change are for more democracy yet: for the abolition of even the residual influence of the monarchy and the House of Lords, for more referendums and for new, directly elected regional bodies. He would, however, recognize this as the same mistake as that made in 1789 by Fox, who supposed that it was still an excess of monarchical power, rather than an uncontrolled popular fever, that was endangering good government and civil order.

Now, as then, it is the institutions that serve to moderate and inform the people's will that need bolstering. If there is to be increasing reliance on the opinion of the man in the street – for want of anyone to put the seemingly illiberal case against reliance upon it – then the man in the street needs to be better educated. He must know the likely consequences of a course of action; he must be conversant with economics and foreign policy; he must be able to balance different objectives and to form his own judgments; he must be able to resist arguments that are whimsical or sentimental. The decency of the man in the street is not qualification enough for statesmanship (as John Major has shown), for there are such things as the street hardly understands. Yet the institutions that might help to make popular opinion more reliable are themselves all succumbing to populism, with standards declining in schools, examining boards, universities, newspapers, libraries, broadcasting and publishing. In every case, quantity is being preferred to quality.

Burke would have been contemptuous of a new kind of abdication of responsibility by our representatives, known as "citizens' juries". These are panels of the public chosen at random by local authorities and other official bodies to adjudicate on particular issues, such as town planning or expenditure priorities. In the name of democracy, this allows the authorities to delegate difficult decisions and to blame someone else if things go wrong. Instead of leaders making informed judgments and standing by the results, it is thought better to rely upon bodies that are anonymous, unqualified, inexperienced, unelected and unaccountable. This is to give a mandate to ignorance. Such panels are most unlikely to be conducive to more a responsible exercise of power. "Woe to that country", writes Burke, that

> considers a low education, a mean contracted view of things, a sordid mercenary occupation, as a preferable title to command. Everything ought to be open; but not indifferently to every man. No rotation; no appointment by lot; no mode of election operating in the spirit of sortition or rotation can be generally good in a government conversant in extensive objects. Because they have no tendency, direct or indirect, to select the man with a view to the duty, or to accommodate the one to the other.
>
> (*Reflections.*)

Rather than put his faith in free-floating democracy, Burke accepted the traditional view that the franchise was necessarily anchored by freehold. Those who were eligible to vote were those who owned land, men of substance. Nevertheless, if those who did not own property were excluded from voting, their interests must not be excluded. "No man", he wrote, "carries further than I do the policy of making government pleasing to the people." This meant that the people's *consent*, their continuing agreement to be governed, must be carried by providing for their well-being. Accordingly, Burke urged that Britain could and should govern the American colonies, or his native Ireland, only with the people's consent, and that if it was lost – as it progressively was in America – then attempting to impose an unwarranted rule was futile and wrong.

This notion of consent is subtler than that of democracy. It is also more liberal and trusting: Dr Johnson's definitions of the noun and verb include "concord, agreement, accord", "joint operation", "to co-operate to the same end", "to yield", "to allow" and "to admit". Democracy is at work only when the people vote, but even if they then repent at leisure, their consent and co-operation persists. We consent to the whole accord of society. We consent to live in families, though we don't exactly elect to; and Burke extended this feeling of loyalty to larger social families, and ultimately to the nation. The rich and tolerant idea of consent, which is related to that of consensus, implies incorporation, concord and continuity. It acknowledges that we do not start from nowhere, but are born into society. The continuance of civil society is, Burke writes,

> under a permanent standing covenant, coexisting with the society; and it attaches upon every individual of that society without any formal act of his own. . . Men without their choice derive benefits from that association; without their choice they are subjected to duties in consequence of these benefits; and without their choice they enter into a virtual obligation as binding as any that is actual. Look through the whole of life and the whole system of duties. Much the strongest moral obligations are such as were never the results of our option.
>
> (*Appeal to the Old Whigs.*)

Consent is more passive than assent; it does not require a popular vote or a specific question; it is an enduring acceptance of and confidence in our inheritance. And consent can answer many needs for which democracy is inappropriate. A police force, for instance, can operate only with consent; but it cannot operate as a democracy.

In consenting to the rule of law, we restrict our freedoms. This, in Burke's terms, is a hallmark of social organization, a triumph of trust. Self-interest is subordinated to an authority which we acknowledge to be greater than ourselves. By throwing in our lot with this arrangement, we can achieve ends that we could never reach alone. We take one of the great imaginative leaps of civilization when we realize that our duties, obligations and laws can be counted – to paraphrase Burke – among our rights, not among our wrongs. We allow that something is more important than we are separately, that society matters more than the individual, and we surrender some primitive prerogatives for our mutual protection. For the sake of other advantages, people may sanction measures which are detrimental to them personally. The taxpayer may disagree with some of the government's spending plans, but he pays up nonetheless, partly to avoid prison, but crucially for the general benefit of living in a civil society. The speeding motorist who pays his fine may not accept the particular judgment, but he agrees there is a need for a Highway Code. Consent is granted not to each discrete act or measure, but to an arrangement. We yield power of decision to others, abide by decisions we may not endorse, and tolerate what we may consider mistaken.

More than a granting of detailed entitlements, consent is a form of prolonged trust. Consenting adults take risks for the sake of the richest of personal and social gains. Except on some American university campuses, where a new contract must be signed for every garment removed, they accept that one thing may lead to another, and may change their lives. And when a couple consent to be married, they are doing more than exchange some narrow permissions; they are, at best, confiding their selves in one another. Similarly, citizens entrust themselves to a commonwealth. Such a consent can be revoked, but this is a calamitous step, not to be taken wantonly.

7

Small is Beautiful

Before Burke, political theorists had been much exercised by questions of prerogative, competency and title. Hobbes, Locke and others had tried to discover what ultimate power, or sovereignty, existed in or over the people. For Burke, however, the abstraction of sovereignty was less congenial than the practicalities of consent and consensus. To say that all authority had originally stemmed from this source or that was to be dogmatic about a past that could not be known; and to say that all authority *ought* to come from a single source was to be impractically doctrinaire. It was also dangerous, for it suggested that the sovereign power – whether king or people – was absolute. Burke regarded authority from above and authority from below as different principles, each important, and thought clashes between them should be avoided, especially if either one was likely to be annihilated.

In discussing the American colonies, Burke remarked that Britain's "sovereignty was not in its nature an abstract idea of unity, but was capable of great complexity and infinite modifications, according to the temper of those who are to be governed and to the circumstances of things". To him, "good-humour in the people", "ordinary tranquillity" and "content" mattered more than any "right" to exercise dominion. In 1774 he said that his ideas for governing the colonies might not satisfy "a refining speculatist, or a factious demagogue", but were "enough surely for the ease and happiness of man".

So in considering constitutional arrangements, he was not bound to this or that theory of sovereignty. Instead, he looked about him and saw how things work in practice, what history had prescribed, and what ministered to contentment. He resisted claims from any side to omnicompetence, and instead synthesized many manifestations of authority, together with a good dose of pragmatism. He argues that authority takes different forms and arises or is vested in diverse bodies and individuals. He writes not of one supreme power, but of "collective sovereignty". For him, the best authorities are generated spontaneously, as people gather freely in small associations for their private, mutual purposes, and agree informally, even instinctively, to rules of behaviour.

In the second of his *Letters on a Regicide Peace*, Burke rejoices in Britain's defiance of a concentrated sovereignty: "The British state is, without question, that which pursues the greatest variety of ends, and is the least disposed to sacrifice any one of them to another, or to the whole. It aims at taking in the entire circle of human desires, and securing for them their fair enjoyment." At the other extreme, people and powers are systematically marshalled when the state aims at a single end – and this will generally be, or become, military.

A proper division and dispersal of authority, Burke saw, produces all the security which human affairs will admit against arbitrary power. Political sovereignty, then, is an unhelpful idea, being itself an absolute presumption. Unfree societies suffer under true sovereignty; free ones are contentedly unsure of where it lies. Britain, for instance, has a sovereign (the monarch), and yet asserts both the sovereignty of Parliament and the sovereignty of the people. What we have most to fear from the European Union is that it is asserting a genuine sovereignty over us: the kind of "unity in design, and perseverance, and boldness in pursuit" that Burke feared in revolutionary France. It is a form of absolutism that has been alien to our traditions and to the spirit of our institutions since the overthrow of the divine right of kings.

It is not the case, as constitutional writers before and since Burke have often assumed, that there must be a single ultimate power in the land (or even invested in a foreign court) which has the final say about everything. To prise constitutions apart to see where the power *really* inheres is to break open the drum to find the source of the noise. The quest for sovereignty, for the single essence, is in vain (as this kind of essentialism generally is). It is asking the wrong question, and all answers are dangerous.

Instead of seeking the rock that is the true political foundation, it is better to regard power as a river. It is fed by many tributaries (the tributaries of the people) but has no single source. We cannot quite define how it begins, but this does not negate its energy. It is always changing, always replenishing, but in practice we know what power is. And it is only in practice that we need to know.

The search for the source of power is based on the mistaken assumption that everything must have a single, definite beginning. But consider ourselves. There is not a moment at which we become fully human, or fully conscious. Like authority, we grow and develop. To try to recall the moment at which the whole contract of society was agreed is like trying to be sure which is our earliest memory: the effort is vain. Even if we could be sure, the child we then were must have had still earlier memories. Our inheritance goes back to the time beyond memory; political systems, like people, do not begin, but develop from an immemorial history. Which is why trying to create a political system anew is like trying to bring a new person into the world as an adult. It cannot be done, for adulthood presupposes memory.

We can learn from Burke's instinct for multiplicity, and his belief that power should be radiated, in what Gibbon called "the scattered rays of civil jurisdiction". At present, our civil and criminal jurisdiction is, instead, focusing more and more on a few higher or sovereign authorities. Yet Burke and Gibbon trust only to a wide range of diverse authorities. Different questions may properly be decided in different ways; there should be matters outside the jurisdiction of the highest of courts or powers because they are the domain of lesser authorities, be they magistrates, local tribunals, school governors, examination boards or the cricket club captain. (How much more pleasing for international cricket to be governed quirkily by the Marylebone Cricket Club than by the ICC!) Those concerned in each issue bind themselves to be governed by the decisions – right or wrong – of particular adjudicators, independently of what anyone else thinks. The cussed ability of such tiny cells of authority outside the state to resist perhaps the full might of government and public opinion is a crucial liberty. The court must be free to make up its own mind on the issue before it, whatever embarrassment may result to managing directors or ministers.

But when distinct jurisdictions and competencies are repeatedly overruled, the basis of authority comes into question. The growing tendency, for instance, for parties at law to appeal beyond the court of first instance – to judicial reviews, higher courts, the Lords, or even foreign bodies – is thwarting the independence and integrity of the lower courts by repeatedly challenging them. Far from guaranteeing our liberties this is gradually diminishing them by making all decisions relative. All too often when a verdict is reported by the newspapers or on television, it is followed by a lawyer saying that his client will be appealing against it. So cases seem to the public never to be settled, the courts are taken less seriously, and the law appears to be forever temporizing. Even if the evidence is overwhelming, the jury is unanimous and the public is satisfied that justice has been done, a wily lawyer can claim that the indictment was poorly drafted, that there was a procedural irregularity, or that the judge "ought" to have directed the court in a way he did not. The lawyer's claim is, at bottom, that the court does not have the moral authority to convict, but only to acquit. And in a society that is widely sceptical about the possibility of any certainty, and where many people consider that everything is subjective, there really is a philosophical problem about standards of proof and reasonable doubt.

A judgment now holds only until the next one overturns it, and the decisions of courts with juries can be reversed by courts without them. But this is a one-way pendulum, for while many of those found guilty have another chance to plead their cases, those acquitted – whether by the first or the tenth court – can never be retried, even if fresh and damning evidence is found. Guilt is made transitory and subjective, and often, during the long, long appeals process, the outrage that surrounds a crime is forgotten or so softened that the perpetrator himself begins to be perceived as a kind of victim (of upbringing, society, the law's delay and so forth). In some cases the acknowledged criminal is then compensated for his ordeal.

Many very long trials result in acquittals which are inevitable, technically correct, and yet less than adequate to the case. Burke's impeachment of Warren Hastings did not, after so many years, conspicuously reach a satisfactory conclusion, although the vast catalogue of Hastings' wrongdoing had demonstrated, as Burke intended, "a *corrupt, habitual*, evil intention". Burke might have had a better chance of convicting if he had not been so overwhelmingly assiduous; yet in a letter to Philip Francis, dated December 10, 1785, before the impeachment had even begun, he wrote that convicting Hastings was "impracticable", and that the important thing for him as the leading prosecutor was to justify himself in the eyes of history.

The Hastings case and some modern fraud trials show that enormously complicated crimes are especially hard to prosecute, because the criminals benefit from deliberately causing confusion and delay. In a trial of years' duration, there is inevitably considerable dissent, uncertainty and forgetfulness, such as must amount to "reasonable doubt". What is unreasonable is the length of the trial. With his extraordinary tenacity, Burke was prepared to devote himself to the impeachment indefinitely, but the defence hoped that the Lords would lose patience and abandon it. Hastings' defence also sought a technical acquittal as cynically as any modern counsel, claiming that the trial could not continue beyond a general election. Burke told the Commons: "It was evidently the aim of Mr Hastings to escape by procrastination, and thus, in the end, baffle the House of Lords." But, he continued, justice must not be thwarted by exhaustion, and accordingly he applied for means to expedite the proceedings.

Modern experience suggests, further, that once a trial is politicized – in the manner, for instance, of the O. J. Simpson case – or turned into a drawn-out symbolic struggle, justice is liable to become a subsidiary consideration. But just as the jurisdiction of the court should be, as far as possible, free from interference, so the demarcation should be clear: a court is not a place to discuss political repercussions or social policy. The involvement of many agencies tends to be inimical to the proper process of law, turning it instead into a charade.

In general, legal technicalities seem to be making it more difficult for cases to be dealt with swiftly, concluded and closed. Ever more safeguards are being built into the system, to protect against this and that recherché injustice. And yet as these clog and confuse the process, justice is less and less understood and seen to be done, and is losing what is vital to it: the people's consent and trust. Of these new mechanisms, we should ask with Burke whether they have "a tendency to convict guilt and clear innocence" or a tendency instead "to provide for the concealment and impunity of guilt".

The true safeguards of British liberty and justice have always been simple, non-technical principles, such as the very idea of justice being "done and seen to be done", or of a jury of one's peers, or of "the truth, the whole truth and nothing but the truth", or the dictum "innocent until proved guilty". Such tenets have become engrained in our language and feelings – rather like, say, the marriage service – and so are intrinsic to our sense of justice. Attempts to replace these homely and trusted ideas by full theoretical structures, capped by an omnipotent Court of Justice ruling in another land, in another language, according to other laws, lead directly to political justice, which is no justice at all. For the European Court of Justice has an extra-judicial, deliberately partial aim. It is devoted, in its own words, to "overcoming the resistance of national governments to European integration". Such political concerns have no place in court. People do not and will not believe that justice is impartially done under a system that is subservient to the will of the government of the moment. Instead, the judgments will be regarded as yet more impositions.

The European superstate to which we have so carelessly and calamitously been subscribed, without our consent, is, in the words of T. S. Eliot, continually "dreaming of systems so perfect that no one will need to be good". This is a mistake in the judiciary as much as in politics. The subordination of British law to that of European institutions threatens the autonomy of our courts. Furthermore, it subordinates the British edifice of case law to a theorizing continental system which draws not upon precedent but upon grand ideals. Instead of looking to particulars, Euro-law seeks to establish judgments with political consequences both sweeping and binding. Too often the intention is less to see justice done than to lay down how people and governments must behave in future. The European Court of Justice and especially the European Court of Human Rights begin with the abstract and inflexible mentality of the written constitution. This supposes that if the law is comprehensive and stringent enough it will be perfect, that it can prescribe for all cases and preclude the need for interpretation, adaptation, local knowledge, sense and decency. It cannot.

Small, limited authorities are more likely to be effective than unwieldy bureaucracies (in which our rulers have placed great faith). The local cell is more likely to understand what is at stake for people. The aggregate of a host of small, manageable decisions, which can be made or modified in the light of previous mistakes, is likely to be happier than the result of an inflexible central plan. For a bureaucracy generally marches to a theory or doctrine, implements the policy it is given and ignores its intuitions and senses. A small, independent enterprise is more likely to be responsive. As Burke wrote, "the errors and deviations of every kind in reckoning are found and computed, and the ship proceeds in her course". (The metaphor is not only vivid but persuasive, for who would steer a ship according to a plan determined in advance and *without* making corrections?)

Small is often beautiful, whereas allowing too few to control too much leads easily to disasters of scale. A small-scale authority has the same virtues as a small-scale building: it makes those inside feel at home, rather than overawed, and those outside can comprehend its form and extent all at once. But confronted with huge, imposing authorities, such as the over-extended, labyrinthine, aggrandizing, impersonal, monumental, baroque Towers of Babel that are the paper-mills of the European Union, the individual feels he has awoken in a Kafka novel or an Escher drawing. He walks an endless corridor of acronyms, past doors marked EEC, EC, EU, EMU, ECJ, EBRD, EMI, ECOFIN, CAP, CFSP, IGC . . . there is no escape. The "architects" of these structures are political vandals, as surely as the builders of high-rise hutches in our cities are destroyers of the human spirit, with its sense of place and rootedness. Yet the European Union is continuing to build itself new palaces and "parliaments" in this style. Politicians have certainly not lost the appetite for building monoliths to glorify themselves, whether they be towers, tunnels, pyramids, stately pleasure-domes or political unions.

Political and concrete brutalism go hand in hand, as they did in Nazi Germany and Soviet Russia. Soulless institutions are housed in soulless buildings. The French Revolution threw up plans for monstrous monuments, such as Bernard Poyet's hospital for 5,000 patients and a 312ft column in honour of "the victories of the nation". Other buildings were projected in the rationalist, inhumane form of perfect cubes or spheres. Fortunately they were not built. Etienne-Louis Boullée, who planned other vast, Soviet-style public buildings, summed up the vainglorious belief that the individual knows best, and can simply discard the accumulated wisdom of tradition: "It isn't by following in the footsteps of others than a creator manages to distinguish himself in the fine arts." But as Burke pointed out when the French revolutionaries first showed the dreadful way, massive constructions that take no notice of people and their habitudes often prove to be mass destructions. An institution should be made for man; man should not be deformed to fit the institution.

For Burke, powers should be not only appropriately scaled, but diversified and distinguished. The government, the nation, the country and society are related but distinct notions, compatible but not identical. And these distinctions too defy the impulse of totalitarianism. Such subtleties make possible, for instance, the idea of Her Majesty's Loyal Opposition: a body critical of the government but committed (supposedly) to upholding the realm. The civil servant works for his department but must not engage in party activity; the judiciary is independent of government: so we insist that functions remain discrete.

Fiercely independent self-governing bodies – consider Oxford and Cambridge colleges, or the Inns of Court, or the merchants' companies – have been the more successful for not having to explain and justify themselves to the state at every turn. Britain's local education authorities, by contrast, have been answerable to everyone in sight and yet do not enjoy widespread confidence.

There is such a thing as too much accountability. An institution that is minutely answerable to outside monitors will always be defensive. It will shun risk and non-conformity, and will instead toe the approved line, whether or not this is appropriate to its situation. It will avoid trouble and controversy rather than pursuing excellence and its independent convictions. An autonomous institution, on the other hand, will find its own ways and means, based on experience and calculated risks. External constraints homogenize institutions rather than cherishing their differences and eccentricities, which – like a diversity of genes – may at some time turn out to be strengths. Pluralism is a hedging of society's bets, whereas uniformity and enforcement – the feminists' wish to ban gentlemen's clubs, for instance – is an arrogant assumption of omniscience. Society benefits from bastions of all kinds, even last ones. When people congregate for their private purposes, they should generally be free within the laws to abide by whatever rules of association they choose, and their agreements or contracts should not be invalidated by outsiders. This principle, however, is little observed now. During a media flurry about the difficulties of celibate priesthood in the Catholic Church, a proponent of change argued that the celibacy rule is "a breach of human rights". This is, once again, to advocate regulation of people's freedom to behave as they choose, or as conscience or custom dictates. It amounts to saying that no one may volunteer to limit his own freedoms in pursuit of a particular goal: self-denial is to be denied. So smug abstraction would trump nine centuries of Catholic practice. It is remarkable how often the supposedly liberal refuse to allow others the liberty of disagreeing with them.

Human institutions, being human, do make mistakes. But not to permit them and their members to face the consequences is to project a perfectibility which is, in Burke's words, "incompatible with human practice". To be sure, there are dangers in allowing private interests to govern themselves, and society has a stake in their affairs too. Burke argued, for example, that Parliament could not ignore the peculations of the East India Company, despite the charter of control over India, because the welfare of millions was involved; but he began from the premiss that private interests should be left alone unless their behaviour was manifestly and systematically in breach of their public trust. There should be an assumption of innocence and a preference for independence, not an assumption that private collaborations are against the public interest and need supervision.

So the autonomy of the specialized bodies which govern many activities should not be reduced by making them minutely answerable or accountable to ever higher authorities (whether local or central government, regulatory agencies or a European court), except upon just and exceptional cause. To do so focuses power in central government, makes a charade of local freedoms, and progressively reduces the number of people who feel they have personal responsibilities in their neighbourhood or field of operation. "Home is where one starts from," wrote T. S. Eliot; "We begin our public affections in our families," wrote Burke.

Some pundits and politicians today believe that because power has become too centralized, new local authorities should be created. This sounds like Burke's argument, but is not. Burke did not believe in separate parliaments for Scotland or Wales, let alone "regional assemblies" for Cornwall and the North of England. These supposedly "local" bodies would have to be imposed from the centre, as nothing of the sort has grown up organically. There is no tradition of such bodies, they do not exist, and there is little evidence of popular demand for them. So this would be an expensive and patronizing farce. Many of those supposedly being represented would resent and resist the interference. The powers of these bodies would be unclear, and would have to be decided and monitored by central government. They would be either impotent or meddlesome.

Local government was once successful and valuable at the level of town and county councils, but these have been corrupted by the growth of the welfare state. What were once local headquarters for a few well-defined services have become fiefdoms controlling enormous budgets and making political decisions about how to allocate patronage among large numbers of supplicants. A good many of the interests claiming public money are dubiously necessary or are committed to social engineering or propaganda in one form or another. This interfering, managerial approach led the conservative commentator Shirley Letwin to write that "liberation from bureaucratic tyrants at the so-called local level is just as essential as at the national level". Local authorities have become increasingly expensive as they have taken over more and more aspects of life. They could merrily spend the entire income of the nation, churning money through taxes and grants and so making every one of us dependent upon them. But this is the opposite of Burke's appeal to the practical good sense of neighbourhoods, the parish priest and the mayor.

Local government today is neither small nor representative. If few people know who their MP is, fewer still know who nominally represents them in local politics. Local election turnouts are tiny, and the voting principally reflects the national performance of the parties – which makes a travesty of accountable democracy. Local administrations can be dismissed, but when they are it is likely to be because of matters over which they have no control. Nor is local government held to account by outside observers. Local politics are considered so complicated, intractable and tedious that few but those directly involved take any interest in them. Local newspapers report what goes on only very selectively, while national newspapers *expect* local government to be corrupt as well as dull. Wrongdoing has to be on an extravagant scale before it merits any coverage. Readers and electors do not have time to care what goes on, and are impatient with the whole business.

Nor is local government forced to be responsible by financial constraints. So high a proportion of local spending is paid for by central taxes that efficiency is very hard to judge (and councils are almost impossible to compare, because their circumstances are never alike). The bulk of the money spent by councils is not raised by them, so they have little incentive to be frugal; yet at the same time, the constraints placed upon them by the size of central government grants are random and inflexible, so they have difficulty budgeting prudently and are forever complaining (often with cause).

This is not the kind of local authority that Burke approved. In his age, local authority did not mean a bureaucracy devolved from above while ostensibly elected from below. It meant the authority of eminent local people – squires, magistrates, priests, schoolteachers – and the summary capacity to settle problems, deal with disputes, punish offenders and look after the needy within a neighbourhood. This sort of effective, respected authority – idealized in the unchallenged hierarchies of *A Midsummer Night's Dream* or *Much Ado about Nothing* – is quite unlike democracy. It is a *modus vivendi* that rests on other principles. It may not always be formally empowered, but is the counterpart of true voluntary charity, as opposed to state-run benefits and social services. It was, and to a limited extent still is, successful in commanding consent, in maintaining a sense of mutual and personal responsibility, and in preventing parochial issues from escalating into major and divisive ones. True local authority extends the scope of private judgment and private life – the loyalties and affiliations that Burke thought basic – whereas local democracy increases the public and compulsory realm, intruding it into everyday life.

There genuinely was a time in Britain in the middle of this century when a reprimand from a teacher or a policeman was enough to put an end to minor trouble among teenagers, and to prevent a recurrence, because it had the implicit backing of parents and society generally. Now, the teacher or policeman is liable to find himself threatened or attacked by the miscreants, or by their parents.

As Janet Daley wrote about a proposed curfew that would allow the police to take children home after dark, there used to be an "informal consensus between responsible, law-abiding adults", which meant that "there was no need for the police to be given the militaristic prerogatives of an occupying power" (*The Daily Telegraph*, June 4, 1996). Burke expressed the general principle in 1791: "Society cannot exist unless a controlling power upon will and appetite be placed somewhere, and the less of it there is within, the more there must be without." Sadly, now, the structures of discipline and the constraints voluntarily observed are so weakened that it seems that the force of law – entailing all the issues of rights, legal warnings, proper procedures, paperwork and appeals – must be exerted in the most trivial of cases. The expenditure is vast, the spectacle offends propriety, the law is demeaned, and suspicion and division are increased.

This kind of heavy-handedness is increasing, as people grow more reluctant to trust each other to behave sensibly and within acceptable bounds. A vicious spiral ensues. A small infringement of proper behaviour is disciplined, but the discipline is not accepted; instead it is appealed against and exaggerated into a breach of "civil rights" (a mother's slap, for instance, becomes assault); so a new, tougher and more formal discipline, quite out of proportion to the problem, has to be imposed upon everyone. This then genuinely does impinge upon the right of people to live in civil harmony. Yet the "civil rights" lobby fails to grasp that it is often the incivility of those it champions that necessitates draconian measures.

As more and more people fail to respect any discipline, the policing of everyone, everything and everywhere becomes more oppressive. Observing the supposed "civil rights" of drunks and prostitutes loitering in King's Cross station has made it impossible for the police to use their discretion to move them on. Instead, the seats on the concourse have been removed. The only seats now are enclosed, guarded and reserved for the use of ticket-holders. So an elderly lady arriving to meet a train is unable to sit down because the freedoms of the anti-social or criminal are considered more important than her frailty. Thus, a fundamentalist, legalistic approach to rights distorts our priorities.

On-the-spot arrangements and discretion generally produce

better results than the unwieldy instruments of law. "Interest, habit and the tacit convention that arise from a thousand nameless circumstances produce a *tact* that regulates without difficulty what laws and magistrates cannot regulate at all," wrote Burke in his *Thoughts and Details on Scarcity*. Typically, he is praising low-key, instinctive and domestic qualities, not public and formal sanctions. This politician wants his work to be done not by committees, public wranglings and statutes, but where possible by the soothing and self-effacing exercise of tact (a word not in use among his cut-and-dried successors). A few pages further on, Burke adds:

> It is one of the finest problems in legislation, and what has often engaged my thoughts whilst I followed that profession, "What the state ought to take upon itself to direct by the public wisdom, and what it ought to leave, with as little interference as possible, to individual discretion." . . . The clearest line of distinction which I could draw, whilst I had my chalk to draw any line, was this; that the state ought to confine itself to what regards the state, or the creatures of the state, namely, the exterior establishment of its religion; its magistracy; its revenue; its military force by sea and land; the corporations that owe their existence to its fiat; in a word, to everything that is *truly and properly* public, to the public peace, to the public safety, to the public order, to the public prosperity. . . Statesmen who know themselves will, with the dignity which belongs to wisdom, proceed only in this the superior orb. . . But as they descend from the state to a province, from a province to a parish, and from a parish to a private house, they go on accelerated in their fall. They *cannot* do the lower duty. . . They ought to know the different departments of things; what belongs to laws, and what manners alone can regulate. To these, great politicians may give a leaning, but they cannot give a law.

Burke puts his trust in leanings, dispositions and the tone of society, rather than in impositions by the state. But now, governments believe they can regulate affairs in the minutest detail, and must interfere in every aspect of life. Britain is reported to have as many as 6,400 "quasi-autonomous non-governmental organizations", with 70,000 members and officials (some with salaries as high as £100,000 a year). In 1994–95 their spending was £60.4 billion. These quangos range from a committee advising on purchase of wine for government drinks parties and a consultative panel on badgers and tuberculosis to the North Hull Housing Action Trust, the Advisory Committee on Conscientious Objectors and the Apple and Pear Research Council. When confronted with a problem, some ministers like nothing better than setting up a committee to look into it. And so, confronted by the problem of these bodies running out of control, they have – yes – set up an independent quango watchdog.

Far from the national life being left in the hands of small civic groups, localities and the kinds of mutual association that form spontaneously, British institutions are being nationalized (organized centrally) and vastly inflated, with almost no consultation or apparent consent. We are overwhelmingly regulated, and denied our discretion. The only man in Britain who begins to understand what is going on, and who tries to unravel the red tape that is asphyxiating the country, is the journalist Christopher Booker, who has worked heroically to expose the disaster, against the opposition of an obfuscating officialdom. In *The Sunday Telegraph* of July 28, 1996, he documented the exponential growth of the threat to liberty under a government nominally committed to reducing restrictions:

> Since April last year the Government has brought in 30 "deregulation orders", which it claims will save businesses £50 million. But in the same period it has issued more than 3,000 new regulations which, on the Government's own estimates, will cost businesses £8,500 million. Since January 1994 the Government has repealed 643 regulations under "deregulation", but in the same period it has issued 8,101 new ones.

Unnecessary regulation, and complex regulation in particular, is morally as well as economically pernicious, for it invites people – or even forces them – to judge for themselves which rules to obey. When there are so many regulations that a small business would have no time to work if it were to comply with them all, the owners will worry more about what they can get away with than about what the law says. And once abiding by the law becomes a luxury, practices become increasingly shady and informal. As rising numbers of us import more duty-free alcohol than we should, or pay in cash to avoid VAT, or distort this or that declaration, the British black economy has grown, so that in 1996 it was estimated to be as high as £85 billion, the size of the social security budget. We become hypocrites about the law, adopting double standards: stringent for others, lax for ourselves.

Giving in to such temptations is typically human and has always been common enough, but in the face of today's myriad incomprehensible restrictions it is more difficult than ever to maintain the standards of honesty that most people nominally subscribe to. The pressures and temptations have increased, and the proliferation of regulations that we do not properly consent to – which never went before Parliament, say, but were imposed as European directives or by a quango – challenges us to cock a snook at petty authority. So our social cohesion is damaged – and government endlessly imagines that it can counter this breakdown by still further intervention: identity cards, curfews, spy cameras, stop-and-search powers, fraud hotlines. But just as condoms do not prevent promiscuity and censorship-chips in televisions will not overcome the problems of copycat violence, so new physical measures and barriers will not solve the moral problems of social breakdown. Modern governments are pitifully prone to the mistake made by the French Assembly: "They renew decrees and proclamations as they experience their insufficiency."

Politicians cannot legislate for higher standards of probity, and may tend to exacerbate the problem if they pretend to. "They *cannot* do the lower duty. . . They ought to know the different departments of things; what belongs to laws, and what manners alone can regulate." Government can, however, give a "leaning" to society, and this, the tone of things, is all-important. Excess of regulation encourages sleaze, as sleaze encourages zealous regulation, and together they establish a tone of low distrust. They move in a circle; they become reciprocally cause and effect. On the other hand, a trust in people's discretion and responsibility "points to virtues".

Burke protested in the Commons on December 15, 1779, that "There is scarce a family so hidden and lost in the obscurest recesses of the community, which does not feel that it has something to keep or to get, to hope or to fear, from the favour or displeasure of the Crown." Now it is not the Crown but the taxes and disbursals of the welfare state, local government, the European Union, the National Lottery and the thousands of regulators that make supplicants or manipulators of us all.

Official interference respects no bounds. Among the recommendations, regulations, decisions and directives of the European

Union are rulings on silkworms, photo-albums (in book-form) and the sound levels of lawn-mowers. Naturally the EU felt obliged to reflect on rear-view mirrors, and the "ecological criteria for the award of the Community eco-label to toilet paper" have to be soft, strong and very long. (Jonathan Swift knew what such documents were best used for.) Everything must be defined, inventoried and regulated, and businesses must simply pay whatever the "Self-Financing Regulatory Agencies" may demand for their masses of certification. The mentality is contagious. The British government even has a programme, with targets, for the reduction of suicides – than which there could scarcely be a less public matter. This penetration of politics into private life has a name, and it is not liberty. These are things, to repeat Burke's words, that ought to be left, "with as little interference as possible, to individual discretion".

8

Manners Makyth Man

Human behaviour is a compound of elements, not susceptible of a single test. Our actions are not simply right or wrong, black or white, but cross-hatched, which is why so many complementary or contending codes have evolved to explain, govern or guide them. Morals, etiquette and laws, for example, all help to regulate behaviour, but they operate on different planes. All three are needed (consider adultery, queue-barging and driving on the wrong side of the road). These various codes are obliquely related, but it is a mistake to try to assimilate or amalgamate them. Beyond the child's vague sense that some things are "naughty" lie the adult distinctions between the impolite, the immoral, the criminal, the dangerous and so on.

According to the first of Burke's *Letters on a Regicide Peace*, "Manners are of more importance than laws. Upon them, in a great measure, the laws depend. The law touches us but here and there, and now and then. Manners are what vex or soothe, corrupt or purify, exalt or debase, barbarize or refine us, by a constant, steady, uniform, insensible operation, like that of the air we breathe in. They give their whole form and colour to our lives." Manners regulate not simply how we behave, but how we think: Johnson's *Dictionary* defines Manners as "character of the mind". They dictate not what is permitted by law, by others, but what we permit ourselves. If we are disciplined by manners, morals and conventions, we may be allowed more legal freedoms. But if conventions that would once have made some things unthinkable are endlessly questioned or flouted (or if, as large numbers of people move from place to place, they are simply not understood), then the rigidity of the law has to be applied. What is not observed voluntarily or as second nature has to be enforced, and the state is strengthened in the name of – but at the expense of – the people. De-moralization is depressing, but it leads also to restrictions and controls which make us ever less free to decide, ever more like automatons.

"Of this the new French legislators were aware," writes Burke;

> therefore, with the same method, and under the same authority, they settled a system of manners, the most licentious, prostitute, and abandoned that ever has been known, and at the same time the most coarse, rude, savage, and ferocious. . . No mechanical means could be devised in favour of this incredible system of wickedness and vice, that has not been employed. . . All sorts of shows and exhibitions calculated to inflame and vitiate the imagination, and pervert the moral sense, have been contrived.
>
> (*Letters on a Regicide Peace.*)

The mechanical means now at the disposal of Hollywood, satellite television broadcasters and every Internet surfer have magnified the danger. If we allow ourselves, for example, to depict and to watch sadistic violence, then it must "by a constant, steady, uniform, insensible operation" begin to corrupt, debase and barbarize our minds and manners. The air we breathe in will be an air of violence. While manners remain, Burke argued, "they will correct the vices of law, and soften it at length to their own temper"; but when manners are corrupted, laws can be relaxed, "as the latter always follow the former, when they are not able to regulate them, or to vanquish them."

"There are gradations in conduct," said Dr Johnson; "there is morality, – decency, – propriety. None of these should be violated by a bishop." Good government should satisfy at least as many criteria as a bishop. To deserve respect and win consent, the practice of rule needs to be accordingly complex, subtle and tactful, and should work through agencies of different kinds. The various authorities of families, schools, ticket inspectors, bank managers and churches, working in their different ways, are as important as the authority of courts and Cabinets.

Ideally, government should be, for instance, representative, wise, decisive, restrained, tolerant, far-sighted and effective. None of these virtues are mutually exclusive, but some are rarely found together – "to unite circumspection with vigour is absolutely necessary, but it is extremely difficult," wrote Burke – so arrangements that can reconcile them are a rare benison. As well as codes of manners, ethics, ritual and etiquette, a well-regulated society needs to harness our feelings of awe, honour, justice, respect, generosity, trust, decorum and loyalty. Such emotions and codes all have a moral value, and Burke believed that "the principles of true politics are those of morality enlarged".

Negative emotions too have their function. Shame, disgrace and taboo, for instance, discourage undesirable behaviour. Today, however, corruption, vice, bankruptcy, violence and even murder can lead to celebrity and vast rewards. In a society where honour matters, keeping one's reputation acts as a spur to virtue and a bridle upon vice. Cassio calls reputation the immortal part of man. But nowadays notoriety is hardly distinguished from fame, and with Iago or a publicity agent to help, dishonour can be turned to advantage. Values can be turned on their heads, but only to the detriment of society.

Human beings have both good and evil instincts, and their leaders should encourage the first and inhibit the second. "Wise legislators of all countries," writes Burke, have always "aimed at improving instincts into morals, at grafting the virtues onto the stock of natural affections." In other words, they appeal to the better parts of man. Government today, however, assumes that people will behave disgracefully and immorally. A "free" condom service for homosexuals is provided on Hampstead Heath, with luminous boxes of them hanging from trees on summer evenings. But the condoms are not free: they are paid for by local taxpayers, many of whom are loath to walk on the Heath when it is attracting hundreds of perverts. These are not quite the sort Burke had in mind when he wrote of "gay, young, military sparks, and danglers at toilets", but they should scarcely be more encouraged.

Nor is lust the only aspect of our baser nature that government panders to. Central government has also encouraged people to be spendthrift, greedy and irrational by setting up a National Lottery of astonishing vulgarity, so further exaggerating the importance of money as people's principle measure of value, and corrupting their various legitimate hopes and aspirations. Burke would have seen a parallel with the Jacobins.

> Your legislators, in everything new, are the very first who have founded a commonwealth upon gaming, and infused this spirit into it as its vital breath. The great object in these politics is to metamorphose France from a great kingdom into one great play-table; to turn its inhabitants into a nation of gamesters; to make speculation as extensive as life; to mix it with all its concerns; and

to divert the whole of the hopes and fears of the people from their usual channels into the impulses, passions, and superstitions of those who live on chances.

(*Reflections.*)

Britain's National Lottery has been shown to be detrimental to the fundraising of particular charities. Its long-term effect is more insidious: the disbursals from its profits give credence to the widespread belief that good causes should be funded institutionally, corporately or nationally, and that they have a "right" to this support. This saps the very idea of charity, the idea of private generosity, not so much of cash as of spirit. True charity involves not just the sentimental pity we feel for the parade of unreachable victims shown on television, but finding an imaginative sympathy with the feelings of others and doing something about it. In this way, suffering and hardship can lead to virtue. Reaching for a credit card doesn't count.

Burke was moved to charity and virtue in 1792, when he heard of the plight of two poor women by the Blackwater in Ireland, and sent them £100 that he could ill afford. He worked for relief of French refugees from the revolution, and at the very end of his life, in 1796, again showed practical compassion when he established a school near Beaconsfield for the orphaned children of French royalists. He persuaded the government to fund it – being in no position to do so himself – and took a detailed personal concern in its management.

True charity is evident in foundations great and small from centuries past throughout Britain: in almshouses, hospitals, schools, colleges and in thousands of specific endowments. Many of these were set up by the rich – albeit often posthumously – for the benefit of the local poor. They offer practical help to the kinds of people visibly in need. Capital sums were left in order to fund benefices forever, but they have been eroded by inflation, and most now appear quaint. The concern to understand and meet practical needs, however, is exemplary and moving – and in feeling quite unlike much of our "charity sector" or bureaucratized welfare state and overseas aid. Because compulsory public welfare has taken over so much of this kind of provision, the aspect of good manners that is private charity has been suppressed. But bureaucracy is much less efficient than the old provision. Whereas the Church asked for a tithe, a tenth of people's income, for charitable purposes, the state demands more than four times that share of the national income. "It would be thought a hard government that should tax its people one tenth part of their time, to be employed in its service," wrote Benjamin Franklin in his notes on "The Way to Wealth". No wonder paying our bloated taxes tends to displace consideration of others.

In *Thoughts on the Present Discontents*, Burke writes that the wise have always "believed private honour to be the great foundation of public trust; that friendship was no mean step to patriotism. . . It was their wish to see public and private virtues not dissonant and jarring, but harmoniously combined". But this must begin with private virtues, not with a dependence upon the state. No political doctrine can offset an absence of goodwill. A civil society must first of all be civil. Unfortunately, people have become less civil as a code of manners which emphasized the claims of others upon us has been superseded by a code of rights which emphasizes instead our claims upon others.

A nation is not just a large aggregate of individuals, and if it is to be properly a nation the people must be prepared sometimes to put something other than themselves first. People should be shown that self-seeking is not their only interest, and encouraged to think of themselves as part of something larger – but not too large. "Men are not tied to one another by paper and seals," writes Burke in the first of the *Letters on a Regicide Peace*. "They are led to associate by resemblances, by conformities, by sympathies." There *is* such a thing as society, and it has many dimensions which are of value, and which are more immediate than the abstractions of state. Loyalty is a noble passion that government ought both to encourage and to harness. But loyalty to universal declarations or international pieties tends to a zealous righteousness which again and again descends into fanaticism. By contrast, a local loyalty, upholding the welfare of a particular people in a particular place, is stable and sustainable. And while people may be loyal to a town or a shire or even a country, they can hardly be so to a continent.

9

The Property of the Nation is the Nation

Writing after the overthrow of France by the revolutionaries, Burke argues that "the pretended Republic" is not France, but a usurpation:

> The body politic of France existed in the majesty of its throne; in the dignity of its nobility; in the honour of its gentry; in the sanctity of its clergy; in the reverence of its magistracy; in the weight and consideration due to its landed property in the several bailliages; in the respect due to its moveable substance represented by the corporations of the kingdom. All these particular *moleculae* united, form the great mass of what is truly the body politic in all countries. They are so many deposits and receptacles of justice; because they can only exist by justice. Nation is a moral essence, not a geographical arrangement. . .
>
> (*Letters on a Regicide Peace.*)

Burke well understood what Herman Melville later described as "the myriad alliances and criss-crossings among mankind, the infinite entanglements of all social things", and he thought that government should represent us not only in isolation, but in our nexus of social relations: as families, as neighbourhoods, as members of social classes, generations, professions, guilds and working groups, as we constitute a school or church or association. Different kinds of involvement in the life of the nation are represented not by the single currency of individual votes, but through different channels, bonds, offices and affiliations. Appropriately, these can be recognized through a panoply of official honours, acknowledging achievement and commitment by means other than financial reward – and thereby resisting the reductive assumption that there is but one scale of values, the monetary. (This upholding of other values is disgustingly mocked when honours are virtually sold to contributors to party funds.) Corporate concerns, whether companies, unions or the Salvation Army, are formed by people for their mutual benefit, but they also help to bind the whole of society. Such groups may own property, and certainly represent interests which have legitimate, autonomous claim to freedom and protection within the state, just as individuals have.

Property, Burke argued, should be represented in the councils of state, because "the property of the nation is the nation". Now, when politicians cant that the nation's biggest assets are its "human resources", this assertion of the central importance of property may sound outdated or provocative, yet it is crucial, for politics (like war) is quintessentially concerned with the disposition of property. Locke had written that "the great and chief end . . . of men's uniting into commonwealths, and putting themselves under government, is the preservation of their property", and Burke insists that far from a culpable materialism, this is one of society's moral supports: "The strong struggle in every individual to preserve possession of what he has found to belong to him is one of the securities against injustice and despotism implanted in our nature."

Property represents stability and certainty. Its security enables people to plan their lives. Without it, or if it is subject to arbitrary confiscation or punitive taxation, or if it is insufficiently protected, there is chaos. "I am in *trust* religiously to maintain the rights and properties of all descriptions of people in the *possession* which they legally hold," wrote Burke in a letter of February 26, 1790. "I do not find myself at liberty, either as a man, or as a trustee for men, to take a *vested* property from one man, and to give it to another, because *I* think that the portion of one is too great, and that of another too small."

The sanctity of private property is for Burke the basis of freedom. Property is what it is proper for individuals (or groups) to control and benefit from, free from interference; but while encroachments upon this private dominion should be resisted, there is also a proper, restrained way for private control to be exercised. For property is also an entail for future generations, and the holder, looking before and after, should acknowledge that his property also has a hold upon him.

Not only land and possessions, but goods such as titles or entitlements – a knighthood, say, or a traditional claim to graze sheep – were comprehended within this idea of property. "By a constitutional policy, working after the pattern of nature," Burke wrote in the *Reflections*, "we receive, we hold, we transmit our government and our privileges, in the same manner in which we enjoy and transmit our property and our lives." The various forms of property were bulwarks against the state, but all of these were threatened by the doctrines of "the most detestable of all revolutions", which devastated land, despoiled houses, despised inherited wealth or rank and denigrated traditional civil rights in favour of grand universal ones. Suddenly, after 1789, everything Burke thought proper was threatened.

Daniel E. Ritchie cogently explains Burke's idea of property in his foreword to the Liberty Fund's useful collection of Burke's so-called *Further Reflections on the Revolution in France*:

> Burke finds an analogy for the political rights enjoyed under the British constitution in the rights that accrue over time to the uncontested holders of lands – "prescriptive" rights. Whereas the revolutionary desires an *im*mediate [unmediated] enjoyment of his liberty and submits to a government only upon sufferance, Burke believed that liberty, proceeding from God as natural law, is mediated through the established, prescriptive laws, usages, and customs of a people. Property rights are the outward and most visible manifestation of prescriptive rights.

Ritchie goes on to say that property rights cannot survive the revolutionaries' continual questioning of authority. If prescription and inheritance are never to be accepted as true title, then no one can ever say how he came legitimately to own anything. All land must once simply have been appropriated. As early as 1755, Rousseau had said that the first man who enclosed a piece of ground was an impostor. This is an argument that everything belongs to the state, and against all private property. No title can ever be secure, as Ritchie writes, "especially if the revolutionaries suppose that the only legitimacy comes from the simple majority of a people at any given moment. But if, over time, a government fulfils the purposes of civil society – namely, the development of man's moral and reasonable nature – then the government (like the property-holder) acquires a prescriptive authority." Property and government are mutually dependent.

Property brings privileges, and in the 18th century one of these was the privilege of voting. At the end of March 1775, Dr Johnson's acquaintance Thomas Campbell confided to his diary reflections on the arguments in Johnson's *Taxation No Tyranny*. "Representation is a right appendant not to persons," he wrote, "but to things, i.e. property." This was not an eccentric view, but the accepted wisdom. However, this "right", or privilege, has been progressively stripped away, and today property has scarcely any direct representation in the councils of state. This may be why the state feels much less compunction about directing how people use their property, is much more prone to compulsory purchases of land and redistribution of wealth, and feels justified in penalizing property-holders by such means as death duties. Property has become correspondingly less secure.

During the American Revolution, the cry went up, "No taxation without representation", and the connection has generally been accepted. And yet almost contradictory principles for taxation and for representation have come to seem immutable. Taxation, it is thought, bears some inherent relation to wealth and must be progressive. Property must pay more. The consensus has been that taxation should increase not only absolutely but proportionally as the wealth of the individual rises (although this is beginning to be challenged, with proposals in the United States for a flat rate of tax). The idea of a poll tax – an equal payment per person – is political anathema or worse. On the other hand, the *only* form of representation many people will now countenance is by poll: one vote per person, without any reference to wealth or property. The idea that representation, like taxation, might be related to property, or any other qualification, is never mooted. The political options, however, might be wider if people knew that principles of representation other than by poll were once accepted. If property is to be taxed, should it not also be represented? If the link between taxation and representation is taken seriously, there may be a case for what Burke calls "representation according to contribution": making at least some aspect of voting power proportional to tax payments (which would mitigate the pain of taxes). Or the tax paid by companies might be considered to warrant some direct representation.

Corporate representation is not unprecedented. Until after the Second World War there were 12 university MPs, for universities were associations then considered – in an age less narrowly democratic – to be of sufficient standing to be represented in Parliament. Other federations of sufficient size, such as trade unions or charities, perhaps with a minimum membership, might also merit seats (not necessarily in the Commons). This would give them a straightforward means of being heard and might reduce attempts to "buy" MPs. Equally, the nation might benefit from their range of expertise.

But particular proposals are a secondary consideration. What should be grasped is that just as there are many forms of taxation, none of which precludes the others, so there are various possible forms of representation, which can be complementary.

Burke argued that various kinds of stake in society, such as those of birthright, land and property, of municipal corporations, local judiciary and administration, the armed forces, capital investment, industry, trade and commerce, personal enterprise and achievement, social influence, the Church, and popular opinion, were all properly represented in government. The state should possess a "variety of parts corresponding with the various descriptions" of which the nation is formed. This is both a realistic assessment of the practicalities of authority and a code of safety, for a state composed of numerous members offers a "joint security", within which it is difficult for any one interest to suppress others. The impulse is the opposite of totalitarian, for it aims to disperse and decentralize power. (Burke's manner and his message were well matched, for as a reader of the *Reflections* cannot fail to notice, he had the habit, as his biographer Bertram Newman put it, "of viewing a matter in as many relations as possible". He was not a politician to be caught out by unintended consequences, but rather pursued, in his rhetoric, every argument he could muster.)

The nation has its warp and weft. And this entails some individuals exercising more than a unitary influence, power through more than one fibre. Just as he denies that all have a right to equal property, Burke denies that all are necessarily entitled to an equal share in the direction of the state. Those who have a part in managing or sustaining a corporate interest have by extension good reason for advancing the national business and prosperity, and have therefore greater incentives to be responsible than people with nothing to lose. Yet what is good for the plutocracy is not necessarily good for the country. The crucial thing is that those with disproportionate power, and there will always be some, should act on behalf also of those with little power, rather than exploiting them.

And the considerations of the powerful must be wider yet. For Burke the Whig, as for his friend Johnson the Tory, society comprised not only those who are alive at a particular moment, but past and future generations too. Taking our forebears and descendants into consideration may at first sound peculiar, but as Roger Scruton has observed, such a concern surfaces "in the thoughts and feelings of ordinary people – as in the environmental movement today". Custom represents the enduring stake in society of our ancestors, and is not easily brushed aside, for it is bigger than we are and forms us to a degree we rarely realize. The past is not over and done with; we cannot cut ourselves off from it. We speak, for instance, its language, live in its houses, listen to its music, profit from its capital. "The past never passes. It simply amasses," writes the American poet Brad Leithauser. Each generation has only limited autonomy. The dead may not vote, but they nonetheless go on influencing our politics. We cannot escape this, and should learn to welcome their investment. "Democrats object to men being disqualified by the accident of birth," wrote G. K. Chesterton; "tradition objects to their being disqualified by the accident of death."

Nor should we be reckless of the future. We should neither betray the dead nor constrain those who are not yet here to protest. The very term "legitimate government" urges the stake of the past and the line of inheritance.

Enoch Powell has said that to explain why the French Revolution did not erupt in England, Burke offered "the principle of prescription", under which "institutions command obedience by reason of their long duration . . . that men are governed in the way they are because they are the sort of people who over a long period of time have come to be apt to be so governed." But such "prescription" is less empty than Powell perhaps makes it sound. Inheritance tends to induce a sense of custodianship, husbandry, trusteeship (though there will always be feckless heirs). As Burke wrote in the *Reflections*, "People will not look forward to posterity, who never look backward to their ancestors." Property affects us, just as we affect it. People who are aware of the processes, cycles and evolution of the past are likely also to have a sense of how cause and effect may shape the future, whereas democracy – especially in the age of the opinion poll and the soundbite – is liable to live only in the immediate and ignorant moment. "The individual is foolish," wrote Burke. "The multitude for the moment is foolish, when they act without deliberation; but the species is wise, and when time is given to it, as a species it almost always acts right."

What matters most in the nation is not the transitory individual, but the endurance of property, society and values. "Individuals pass like shadows; but the commonwealth is fixed and stable."

10

A Permanent Body of Transitory Parts

Burke saw that society and government were knit together by many threads of allegiance, authority and obligation. Overlapping interests were served, and this overlapping – so untidy to the officious mind – was a form of protection, for disparate principles were always represented. Temporally, balancing the short-term occupants of an elected chamber with the entrusted inheritance of the Lords and the lifetime incumbency of the monarch, the figurehead of the age, gave the security of unsynchronized cycles. At a time of crisis or change in one estate, the others could offer continuity. In this manner, in 1688-89, the constitution was upheld and peace was maintained through the most momentous of changes: the removal of a King. In a conserving revolution, the line of succession was changed, but not the institution of monarchy. A revolution was, Burke wrote, "not made, but prevented".

> Our political system is placed in a just correspondence and symmetry with the order of the world, and with the mode of existence decreed to a permanent body composed of transitory parts; wherein, by the disposition of a stupendous wisdom, moulding together the great mysterious incorporation of the human race, the whole, at one time, is never old, or middle-aged, or young, but, in a condition of unchangeable constancy, moves on through the varied tenor of perpetual decay, fall, renovation, and progression.
>
> (*Reflections.*)

Perhaps this is the kind of thing Isaiah Berlin had in mind in 1978, in his essay on "Nationalism", when he accused Burke of writing "florid and emotive prose". In such passages, Burke is not just a statesman, author or pamphleteer, but a man of profound human compass, seeing life steadily and seeing it whole, as the great poets have. (Coleridge hailed him as "almost a poet".) Burke's description is not of a political system solely, but of our proper place in the cycles of mortality. His "decay, fall, renovation, and progression" are akin to Tennyson's "Tithonus":

> The woods decay, the woods decay and fall,
> The vapours weep their burthen to the ground,
> Man comes and tills the field and lies beneath,
> And after many a summer dies the swan.

This is an ordinance with its various life-cycles – the seasons, the life of man, the geological ages – and Burke senses that the body politic ought to respect its own "great mysterious incorporation". The permanence of the world is built on the principle of change. Government, like a family, "is never old, or middle-aged, or young", but a sort of combination.

Geographically, Burke saw a different kind of overlapping, also making for stability, in the organic pattern of representation. The incongruence of Britain's parishes, boroughs, districts, counties, regions, wards and constituencies militated against local tyrannies. If the alderman, the magistrate, the priest, the councillor and the mayor each have different territories, they cannot easily act together against the people – or be controlled from outside.

Accordingly, Burke was witheringly critical of the revolutionary attempt to divide France into perfectly square departments, communes and cantons, within which all types and tiers of administration would coincide. This was to ignore the dictates of topography, the features and contours of the landscape, which Montesquieu had taught Burke to respect. It was an attempt, too, to annul history, by discarding the ancient names of streets and communes. Burke saw not only absurdity, but danger in this "geometrical constitution" with its obedient hierarchy. Instead of districts with their traditional attachments and affinities arranging to send representatives to larger authorities, the French state wanted to dictate from the centre the lines on which people were to be divided and ruled. Burke defended the untidy, contingent accommodations of ages against the streamlining impulse which jettisons a kind of resilience it does not even recognize. By analogy today, Britain's several police forces, with their local loyalties and almost regimental pride and independence, are preferable to a single state police (which could more readily be used to bring about a police state). Better that authorities should be peers and rivals, and so check each other – being able even, on occasion, to investigate one another – than that there should be a monolith.

It is no coincidence that the Prime Minister who felt it necessary to subjugate Britain to a European authority, so attempting to give away the whole of the national property, was noted also for re-arranging the counties and for "rationalizing" our currency, our weights and our measures. He stopped short only of decimalizing the calendar, unlike the French revolutionaries with what Burke called their "gipsy jargon". Given that the boundaries, the currency and imperial measures had grown up, prescriptively, over hundreds of years, it is hard to imagine how the British people could have consented to such sudden changes, even if they had been asked. It would entail giving away their inheritance and changing their very selves. Could any Yorkshireman ever become a Lancastrian?

Burke explains in the second of his *Letters on a Regicide Peace*, that the old governments of Europe have evolved, and not been imposed according to grand schemes.

> The states of the Christian world have grown up to their present magnitude in a great length of time, and by a great variety of accidents. . . Not one of them has been formed upon a regular plan or with any unity of design. As their constitutions are not systematical, they have not been directed to any *peculiar* end, eminently distinguished and superseding every other. The objects which they embrace are of the greatest possible variety, and have become in a manner infinite. In all these old countries the state has been made to the people, and not the people conformed to the state.

Following Montesquieu, Burke understood that different geography and national evolutions entailed different details in the arrangements of government. By contrast, the new dissectors thought they could find a single, universal and impregnable answer to all political problems (and so reach the end of history). William Godwin wrote: "There must in the nature of things be one best form of government which all intellects, sufficiently roused from the slumber of savage ignorance, must irresistibly be inclined to approve." Socialism has always thought of itself this way, but as Burke expected, the talk of rousing and of irresistibility led, when universal approval was not forthcoming, to violent attempts to impose this "best form of government", the perfect constitution, which could be proclaimed anywhere and everywhere. With its failure of humility, the 18th-century search for an ultimate solution dreadfully prefigured the 20th century's attempt to impose solutions.

Rather than endorsing any pure theory of entitlement to govern,

Burke acknowledges "the various anomalies and contending principles that are found in the minds and the affairs of men", and this is their strength: "From hence arises, not an excellence in simplicity, but one far superior, an excellence in composition." So he assesses the advantages and dangers of different ways to govern a nation, in the belief that the advantages can be compounded and the dangers offset. He judges not by the degree of conformity to an abstract ideal, but by the happiness and consent of the people. Democratic voting is one of the means of establishing consent, but it is not a perfect means, for it has characteristic shortcomings. By now these have been exacerbated by the increase and concentration of media power, and the professionalization of what Burke called the "electioneering arts". With millions of pounds (or billions of dollars) being spent at modern elections, we may well wonder whether the corruptions that Hogarth satirized in the 1750s have been swept away or merely updated. But even if elections were entirely just, democracy as a system has failings. The rule of democracy alone would be like the rule of law unmoderated and uninflected by morality or manners.

Yet now even people who understand the old strength of Britain's pluralist constitution go on wishing to simplify it. The historian David Starkey describes the situation accurately, but for one thing:

> The old British constitution, whose perfections were universally admired, was a pre-democratic one. Its balance depended upon the fact that only one element, the House of Commons, was democratic or elective. The Crown was monarchical; the House of Lords, aristocratic. The result was an ideal compound of classical political thought in which the rule of one was exactly combined with the rule of the few and that of the many.
>
> In the American adaptation of the British constitution, all three elements, represented respectively by the president, the Senate and the House of Representatives, were made elective and hence given democratic legitimacy. In Britain, however, only the House of Commons was. This robbed first the Crown and then the Lords of political legitimacy. . .
>
> (*The Sunday Times*, July 21, 1996.)

If the "ideal compound" of the old British constitution produced a balance of "perfections" which were "universally admired", why is

Starkey not anxious to return to it? Because he complacently assumes, without troubling to argue, that the only kind of legitimacy is democratic: the mistake against which Burke strained every sinew.

We should no more reduce government to a single faculty than we would assert the superiority of sight and forgo the other senses. The majority's preference is one faculty, but we should respect the roles also of, say, seniority, learning, tradition. Each faculty needs to be modulated by others, because as Burke wrote, "Everything is good or bad, as it is related or combined."

If we ask what right any body may have to take part in government when it is not directly elected, the answer is that while the popular vote represents the immediate wishes of the people, society is more than this. It depends upon lasting disciplines and understandings which individuals – or even a whole generation – may not possess or acknowledge. Our technological society, for instance, relies upon the genius of Alexander Graham Bell and John Logie Baird, and although the present generation grasps their technical knowledge, it might be unable to replicate the conditions which brought about their insights. Left to our own devices, without theirs, we might not be able to invent the telephone and the television.

No individual wholly grasps how Heathrow Airport fulfils its function. The safe and successful planning of thousands of flights is the result of a collaboration not only between people with diverse skills, but across time. Many of the essential structures – from the terminal buildings to the flight numbering conventions – were established by people no longer on the site. The operation also depends upon the teamwork, years ago, of engine designers, logistics experts and computer programmers. The airport can only function by employing this inherited wisdom. When a member of one of its various staffs leaves, someone else must be trained into the job, and he in turn will develop and adapt it. The operation expands organically, and responsibilities divide like cells. Custom and practice are passed on.

In the same way, the transmission of a nation's accumulated political wisdom is a requisite for the working of its institutions. The principle of stability, even sluggishness, which Burke associates with heredity, is essential to preserve that past knowledge and expertise which the present generation may not share but still, unwittingly, depends upon. Heathrow could not be run by polling all of its personnel to reach decisions: their expertise is too fragmented. It works because of the continuity of the operation. Equally, the workings of a nation and the conventions it relies upon require many different faculties to be exercised, which are not fully understood by the mass of people.

11

Take But Degree Away

The outbreak of revolution in France prompted excited debate in Britain. On the fall of the Bastille in July 1789, Fox wrote in a letter, "How much the greatest event it is that ever happened in the world! and how much the best!" But only seven prisoners had been found there, and one of Burke's letters better anticipates the judgment of later historians: "As to the destruction of the *Bastille*, of which you speak, we both know it was a thing in itself of no consequence whatever." In the initial exhilaration of the revolution, Burke kept his head while all about him, and still more in France, were losing theirs. For him, well-conducted politics was not visionary, exciting and inflammatory, but cautious, gradual and patient. Yet as time went on, his anti-revolutionary polemics became increasingly impassioned.

Reflections on the Revolution in France had an immediate effect on many in Britain, and not least in Parliament, who had been rapturous or undecided about the revolution in its first year. When it was published, Burke's assessment was utterly different from any other, but it soon dampened British ardour for the slogans of Paris, which had been endorsed at first by both Fox and Pitt. The book set the scene for a grim disillusionment, as Burke's predictions of chaos and the rise of a military dictator were fulfilled. This was the change of heart recorded most famously in *The Prelude*, into which Wordsworth belatedly wrote a passage in praise of Burke.

Analysis of political movements in retrospect is easy enough, but no one has ever matched Burke in anticipating the repercussions of a great event, in both sweep and detail. As Conor Cruise O'Brien writes, the word "clairvoyant" is scarcely too strong. Still the repercussions continue, and still Burke's book is the best guide to them, as well as the earliest history of the revolution.

Burke was not xenophobic. He loved and honoured France, "a generous and gallant nation" which he had visited at least four times and knew well. French writers and statesmen visited him and stayed at Beaconsfield. After the outbreak of the revolution, he maintained contact with numerous French correspondents, and welcomed several émigrés to his home. He was at war not with the nation but with an ideology, and he felt not triumph but pity for the deplorable wreck of France herself. "The truth is," he wrote in 1793 in his *Remarks on the Policy of the Allies* "that France is out of itself – The moral France is separated from the geographical. The master of the house is expelled, and the robbers are in possession." The "*corporate people*" of France were in exile.

When he described the "Regicide Republic" of France as "an *armed doctrine*" – a phenomenon unprecedented except by religious crusades – he foresaw a new kind of prolonged conflict, not just between states but between freedom and whole systems of tyranny. Consequently, many of his remarks on the "Regicide Peace" apply as well to the Russian Revolution as to the French, as well to the appeasement of Hitler as to the appeasement of Carnot. "It is a controversy", he wrote in his *Remarks on the Policy of the Allies*, ". . . between the proprietor and the robber; between the prisoner and the jailor; between the neck and the guillotine."

Burke helped Britain to avoid revolution, but the nation nevertheless went on to make what he would have considered many of the same mistaken concessions as France to destabilizing ideas, albeit with less bloodshed. These ideas promised emancipation, yet we are still trying to find ways to live with their liberating effects.

In the systematizing age of the great French *Encyclopédie*, there was a temptation to assume that all phenomena were comprehensible, and that everything would one day be classified, catalogued, explained, perfected and controlled. The French mathematician and philosopher Condorcet argued in his *Progrès de l'esprit humain* (1794) that in the coming epoch all inequalities would be destroyed, and human nature itself would be perfected by reason. Anticipating Marx, he wrote of society as progressing logically through definable stages towards an inevitable utopia. But Burke saw that social affairs were, on the contrary, so delicate, elaborate and shifting as to defy definitive description. "A common soldier, a child, a girl at the door of an inn, have changed the face of fortune, and almost of nature," he wrote in the first of the *Letters on a Regicide Peace*. Two centuries before chaos theory suggested that cause and effect are impossible to calculate even in the physical world, he argued that the interactions between men and institutions (and between past, present and future) were quite different from mathematical propositions and philosophical abstractions.

> Far from any resemblance to those propositions in geometry and metaphysics, which admit no medium but must be true or false in all their latitude, social and civil freedom, like all other things in common life, are variously mixed and modified, enjoyed in very different degrees, and shaped into an infinite diversity of forms according to the temper and circumstances of every community.
>
> (*Letter to the Sheriffs of Bristol*, 1777.)

The revolutionaries taught men to be philosophical iconoclasts and to blame human institutions for the miseries of life. They believed society could begin again, as though with a *tabula rasa*, and could disregard all that time had made venerable. Burke was aghast: "I cannot conceive how any man can have brought himself to that pitch of presumption," he wrote in the *Reflections*, "to consider his country as nothing but *carte blanche*, upon which he may scribble whatever he pleases."

As far back as his *Letter to the Sheriffs of Bristol*, Burke had rejected the abstractions of contemporary political theorists, which the French Revolution was to try to implement. "I was persuaded that government was a practical thing, made for the happiness of mankind, and not to furnish out a spectacle of uniformity to gratify the schemes of visionary politicians."

Rousseau, Paine and their followers encouraged people not to reform and refine the constituents of culture, but to abandon them and to learn directly from "nature". However, this idea, in which the Romantics were to invest so heavily, is dangerously vacuous. It is, say the *philosophes*, obvious that in an uncorrupted state of nature all men would be equal. Yet it is only human institutions that can construct anything like equality before the law. Without such disciplines, men are like children uncorrupted by the most basic training. "Nature" is brutally inequitable, and fits only a few to survive. In any case, the hypothesis of a human nature preceding society is a myth, for man is a gregarious and creative animal. The Hobbesian idea of man in a state of nature – isolated, self-centred and hostile – had been challenged by Montesquieu. This primitive individual never existed, and to appeal to him entails wishing to destroy, or to deconstruct, our social institutions.

Two centuries on, however, we have not escaped deceptive appeals to what Burke called "a pretended natural equality in man", and to the correlative of these, "the rights of man" (now renamed "human rights"). These revolutionary chimeras wrought havoc in the 1790s and wreak havoc still. But is it better that people be ruled with numerical justice, or that they feel they are ruled fairly? Is it better that they have their legal entitlement – the kilo of flesh that every litigious Shylock demands – or that they be content? Better that they have equal shares, or that they be without envy? In private life, we learn sooner or later that it is better to give than to receive; Burke taught such generosity as a political principle. Happiness is achieved by concession, and most people "choose rather to be happy citizens, than subtle disputants". But is it still so?

Attempted equality is unfair, and leads to unhappiness and dissent. William Bradford's history *Of Plimouth Plantation*, written 1630–51, poignantly describes a well-meaning attempt by American settlers to live by communal, egalitarian rules, and the not dishonourable reasons for their failure:

> The experience that was had in this common course and condition, tried sundry years, and that amongst godly and sober men, may well evince the vanity of that conceit of Plato's and other ancients, applauded by some of later times; – that the taking away of property, and bringing in community into a commonwealth, would make them happy and flourishing; as if they were wiser than God. For this community (so far as it was) was found to breed much confusion and discontent, and retard much employment that would have been to their benefit and comfort. For the young men, that were most able and fit for labour and service, did repine that they should spend their time and strength to work for other men's wives and children, without any recompense. The strong, or man of parts, had no more in division of victuals and clothes than he that was weak and not able to do a quarter the other could; this was thought injustice. The aged and graver men to be ranked and equalized in labours, and victuals, clothes, etc., with the meaner and younger sort, thought it some indignity and disrespect unto them. And for men's wives to be commanded to do service for other men, as dressing their meat, washing their clothes, etc., they deemed it a kind of slavery, neither could many husbands well brook it. Upon the point all being to have alike, and all to do alike, they thought themselves in the like condition, and one as

> good as another; and so, if it did not cut off those relations that God hath set amongst men, yet it did at least much diminish and take off the mutual respects that should be preserved amongst them. And would have been worse if they had been men of another condition. Let none object this is men's corruption, and nothing to the course itself. I answer, seeing all men have this corruption in them, God in His wisdom saw another course fitter for them.

Yet despite practical failures, utopian projects to achieve equality have been attempted down the ages, with little success and much acrimony. "In this," Burke wrote, "you think you are combatting prejudice, but you are at war with nature." He thought the idea of an equal society naïve, and strove for that more subtle, more free thing, an equitable one. In a letter to John Bourke in November 1777, he wrote:

> The idea of forcing everything to an artificial equality has something, at first view, very captivating in it. It has all the appearance imaginable of justice and good order . . . [but] I am, for one, entirely satisfied that the inequality, which grows out of the *nature of things* by time, custom, succession, accumulation, permutation, and improvement of property, is much nearer that true equality, which is the foundation of equity and just policy, than anything which can be contrived by the tricks and devices of human skill.

To insist that "all men are equal", or have a "right" to be so, is to encourage vain expectation and so make a grievance out of the inequality that is an aspect of the human condition. As James Fitzjames Stephen wrote a century later: "To try to make men equal by altering social arrangement is like trying to make the cards of equal value by shuffling the pack." People are not equal, and no one – not a saint nor a communist – behaves as if they were. Yet to recognize that we have different abilities and preoccupations, different values and different stations in life should not entail injustice, unkindness or lack of sympathy. On the contrary, it should engage our imagination and respect, and remind us of our interdependency. The more privileges and interests we have, the more people we rely upon and interact with. The more we understand this indebtedness, the more we should feel our responsibilities. When privilege leads to arrogance, there has been a failure of education and imagination – a failure not to prevent inequality, but to acknowledge the human value of others. For since personal equality cannot be enforced by law, inequality must be tempered by codes of decency.

A society that understands inequality and class is one in which no one is untouchable or unjustly set apart, and in which mutual respect is part of normal discipline and manners. Manifestations of class can be absurd or obnoxious, and can provoke animosity. But class itself is inevitable. What a harmonious and mature society seeks to avoid is not class, but class provocation, whether through the thoughtless and self-destructive behaviour of the privileged, or the stirring up of resentment by agitators. A nation at ease with itself is not one without class, but one that is not filled with class guilts and jealousies. Burke was quick to deplore those who made it their business to arouse class hatred. "It is fatally known," he wrote in one place, "that the great object of the Jacobin system is to excite the lowest description of the people to range themselves under ambitious men, for the pillage and destruction of the more eminent orders and classes of the community." And in another: "They pretend that the destruction of kings, nobles, and the aristocracy of burghers and rich men, is the only means of establishing an universal and perpetual peace. . . Under any circumstances this doctrine is highly dangerous, as it tends to make separate parties of the higher and lower orders, and to put their interests on a different bottom."

One of the rallying calls of Paine the demagogue was for the Common Man to distrust those who led or governed him. Only Paine himself, as the supposed embodiment of Common Sense (the title of one of his books, and the two words with which he habitually signed his name), was to be exempted from this distrust. Dissatisfaction and dissent were essential to his politics. On the other hand, for Burke (a man of uncommon sense), a precondition of concord and consent was that the different ranks of men should not feel themselves at odds, but should recognize their reciprocal interests. At the very least, all benefit from the maintenance of a peaceful, regulated civil society.

"Every man is rich or poor," wrote Dr Johnson in *Rambler* No 163, "according to the proportion between his desires and enjoyments; any enlargement of wishes is therefore equally destructive to happiness with the diminution of possession; and he that teaches another to long for that which he shall never obtain, is no less an enemy to his quiet, than he who robs him of part of his patrimony." Thomas Paine, an enemy of quiet, enlarged the hopes of many without the means to satisfy them. He was, as Burke put it, stirring up the people to "improper desires".

Class divisions are often said to be especially acute in Britain, but what this means is hardly examined. Class in Britain is a complex mix, akin to our rich constitutional mix: it too has different forms and principles. Some members of the Royal Family are said not to have much class – even to be vulgar. So class is not simply to be gauged by rank or wealth or fame, though these may be components. In Britain, we assess each other by a multitude of criteria, including profession, taste, address, qualifications, accent, breeding, intelligence, dress, schooling, wealth, upbringing, table-manners and friends. Which of these matters to an individual varies, and this is in itself a freedom. We feel comfortable to be very different kinds of people within a single society, and we explicitly value and dedicate ourselves to many things other than money, such as a wealth of causes, hobbies and studies. Accordingly, Britain is a conspicuously more cosy, diverse and deeply rooted society than some younger countries, where anything can be despoiled if the accountants dictate it. Britain still has some sense of the particular place, some style of its own, and some resistance, though not enough, to the universal architecture and values of the cosmopolitan world of finance and trade. To an extent, the British are contentedly divided into classes by what they are accustomed to. One group in society does not wish to live like another, or to move up into a "higher" class. People are generally proud of their accents, which demarcate class as well as region, and by and large like things – domestic things, red phone boxes, little hamlets, local eccentricities, political anomalies – just the way they are.

In Britain, some people choose to judge and be judged by the old school or club tie they wear, or to luxuriate beneath a family coat-of-arms. Others are free to disregard these vanities – or scorn them – and to assess their peers by their cars, or their dogs, or their ability to grow prize pumpkins, or play the piano, or understand Edmund Burke. People are admired and respected for many things, and show their class or lack of it in many ways. This is not to deny that many attributes of class often go together, but it does mean that there are diverse ways to pursue happiness or to "better oneself". Not every judgment is made on the basis of income, as is liable to be the case in a country where egalitarianism pretends that you're better than no one and no one is better than you. After all, we each enjoy (perhaps need) the vanity of believing that we *are* better, if only in the egg-and-spoon race. And a country where people can choose in which of many races to run can have more winners: for diverse reasons more of us can enjoy that crucial thing, self-esteem.

Our perception of inequality is one of the instinctive sources of respect for authority. We admire people, achievements or collaborations that are beyond our personal scope. We respect surpassing valour, strength, wisdom, beauty and other qualities, and are readily willing to acknowledge their fitness to take a lead – unless our feelings are warped into malice and envy. In 1807, William Hazlitt summarized the importance of a natural respect:

> . . . it is natural to think highly of that which inspires us with high thought, which has been connected for many generations with splendour, and affluence, and dignity, and power, and permanence. [Burke] also conceived that by transferring the respect from the person to the thing, and thus rendering it steady and permanent, the mind would be habitually formed to sentiments of deference, attachment, and fealty, to whatever demanded its respect: that it would be led to fix its view on what was elevated and lofty, and be weaned from that low and narrow jealousy which never willingly or heartily admits of any superiority in others. . .
>
> ("Eloquence of the British Senate".)

Most civilizations have taken it for granted that parents should control their children, that the old should guide the young and the wise instruct the ignorant, that the well-born should govern the lowly, and the strong should lead the weak. They may have been complacent or unjust, but historically it is the egalitarian ideal that arose in Burke's day that is the aberration.

Authority, after all, is not only the legal power to enforce obedience, but a personal quality commanding respect. It must be earned as well as asserted. To say that someone is an authority is to acknowledge an eminence attained by expertise, and among those of our legislators with a proper title to such eminence, many are lords. But if today we are not led by people of distinction and conviction, it is partly because the political class has lost its nerve and become afraid of distinctions. We may say to them, as Burke did to the French in the *Reflections*, "you have industriously destroyed all the opinions, and prejudices, and, as far as in you lay, all the instincts which support government". Politicians are reluctant to claim any superiority that might qualify them for office. Only popularity in the gross counts now.

"Discrimination", which was once allied to "discernment" and "distinction", has become almost exclusively a pejorative term. This may seem a generous impulse, giving the benefit of the doubt to those who are untried. But frustrations are certain to increase the more we believe in egalitarianism, for the doctrine implies that our superiors, at work for instance, can never truly be superior, but must always have gained advancement for reasons other than merit. Too often we do find that jobs are filled from a closed circle and for irrelevant reasons (and Burke looks at fault here for nepotism in appointing his relations to the Pay Office); but to believe that no one *could* ever deserve higher status or truly earn more than ourselves would be to feel permanently aggrieved. To institutionalize cynicism rather than respect is a dangerous expedient.

Although we now put ourselves in specialist hands in almost every area of life, few question the assumption that in politics the ordinary Joe knows best. Consequently MPs aim to appear as ordinary as possible. But this recent dogma overturns the belief of all previous human history, that leadership comes from the extraordinary few, not the unexceptional many. It is certainly a less intuitive, more theoretical position than that of Burke, who wrote that "force of character" must ever be inspired from above.

Now, however, a nominally Conservative Prime Minister advocates a "classless society" – as though there could be such a thing. Gone, then, is the wish to elevate the minds and aspirations of the people; gone is the hope of setting an example to be emulated, leading people towards what they never knew themselves capable of; gone is the confidence that some values should be upheld and extended, even if their importance is not apparent to the majority. Conspicuous intellect is thought by some to be suspect in a minister. A Prime Minister aims not to prove his outstanding gifts, but to show that he is unremarkable. Either this supposed Conservative believes that the absence of any social scale is the only form of justice, or else he feels obliged to say so in the name of democracy. "Take but degree away," writes D. J. Enright sardonically of this naïve hope, "and social concord will prevail."

12

Reflections of Inequality

It is self-evidently true that we are born unequal. Most obviously, physical handicaps make some people less than equal, though the law properly tries to ensure that they are treated as equally as possible. But inequality is evident in every aspect of life, from athletics to musical aptitude. Most genetic advantages have to be realized by application, but some, such as beauty, may be enjoyed without effort and so – like social status – bring little feeling of achievement.

Some children are born into affluent, cultured families, others have to struggle to make their own way. Some sons and daughters live in the shadow of famous parents, perhaps quite willingly (like Burke's son) or perhaps miserably (like Churchill's). For all of us, the circumstances in which we are born inevitably have a bearing on our lives, but the financial aspect is not usually the most important or formative. Some children have the greatest of all advantages, the love of their parents; others are unwanted.

Those who are born great inherit not just wealth and titles, but responsibilities to live up to. An aristocrat who is bequeathed a stately home full of magnificent works of art has a family duty to the estate, and probably to local people and the nearby village or town as well. He also has a larger cultural duty. Born into what should be a life of responsibility and husbandry, he is less free than most of us. We may envy the Prince of Wales or the son of John Paul Getty in several ways, but their lives are not entirely their own. Their birth will not suffer them to be private. More than ours, their lives' trajectories are determined by their families. They have a mass of interests to look after, few of them personal. They must consider the well-being of many people, and are custodians of treasures which they hold in trust for the public and for future generations. The greater the privilege, the greater the duty. And it is to the benefit of us all that there should be a class of people who have grown up putting these considerations before their personal wishes, as, for instance, the Queen has done. Their security means that they are able to consider the broader meanings of wealth and to think about their decisions' lasting consequences for, say, the future of the countryside or of the country itself. With them, financial considerations need not always outweigh other values, such as the aesthetic, scholarly, conservationist or scientific. Totting up the fortune of the Duke of Devonshire so as to foment jealousy misses the point about the Duke of Devonshire. He should and will be judged not by statistics, but by how much good he is able to do. Such individuals, as Burke wrote in a letter to the Duke of Richmond, have an exemplary public role:

> The immediate power of a D. of Richmond or a Marquess of R[ockingha]m is not so much of moment but if their conduct and example hands down their principles to their successors; then their houses become the public repositories and offices of record for the constitution, not like the Tower or Rolls Chapel, where it is searched for and sometimes in vain in rotten parchments under dripping and perishing walls, but in full vigour and acting with vital energy and power in the characters of the leading men and natural interests of the country.
>
> (Written *post* November 15, 1772.)

Many of man's noblest achievements and monuments would have been impossible without a small class of the luxuriously rich. Wealth enables people to raise their eyes above the functional and immediate, gives them time to contemplate and explore their situation, to wander in the realms of gold – of philosophy, science and art. The Parthenon, the Sistine Chapel, *The Last Supper*, the Taj Mahal, Columbus's voyages, Galileo's observations, Oxford University, Haydn's quartets, the British Library and the theory of evolution are all products of concentrated wealth, which allowed the leisured to dream, invent, commission and act as patrons. Had wealth been more evenly distributed, they would not have been possible. But the benefits of such imagination are not restricted to the few. To begin with, the funding of great projects gives work to many. It liberates and enables the truly creative (Michelangelo and Donatello, rather than the Medici family). Then the products, although they may be privately enjoyed for a generation or more, outlast their time and eventually become part of the capital stock of humanity. Whether they like it or not, by investing or spending their money, the very rich become benefactors of us all.

Many grand projects have been and are today paid for either by market forces and public demand (such as Shakespeare's plays) or by governments (such as space exploration), but there remains a role for individuals or families, who can back their intuitions or whims or friends against the scorn of the world. There is a place for the unanswerable and eccentric.

The noble project of government also has a role for those who, as Burke wrote in a massive sentence in his *Appeal to the Old Whigs*, "stand upon such elevated ground as to be enabled to take a large view of the widespread and infinitely diversified combinations of men and affairs in a large society" and for the professors "of high science, or of liberal and ingenuous art". The national councils need representatives of the finer things in life, its ideals and aspirations, to balance the representatives of hardship and common woes, the calculators and the cost-counters.

There are true aristocrats, men and women of liberality, talent and wide understanding. Their distribution is random and unfair, and the House of Lords is only a simulacrum of this aristocracy. Yet the peers are a healthy reminder that life deals each of us a hand, and that we must make the best of it, not waste our precious time in complaining that we ought to have other cards. We should be provident with what providence gives us.

Hereditary lords inherit both the privilege and the burden of greatness, and are a useful counterbalance to politicians who sedulously achieve their eminence. For while the House of Commons displays the virtues and drawbacks of political professionalism, the hereditary lords display the complementary virtues and drawbacks of amateurism. In some respects, the peers may be more typical of the people than the Commons, for they are not self-selected politicians; and as D. B. Somervell put it, "The House of Lords *should* be an irrationally constituted body, like a jury". The virtue of the Lords is not that they are rationally chosen, but that they tend to make the exercise of power wiser and more liberal.

The House of Lords is more diverse than the Commons, with a wider range of experience in private life than that rather middle-class chamber. Magnus Linklater has described the benefits of their expert advocacy:

> The strength of the House of Lords lies in the fact that its members represent nobody but themselves. They are in a sense an assembly of vested interests. . . When a landowning peer from the

> north of Scotland ventures down to Westminster to speak about forestry, he may well be accused of a conflict of interest since he probably owns several thousand acres of trees. But he is also speaking with a first-hand knowledge which is likely to be denied an MP from Penge. Viscount Thurso . . . recalled that his father, who owned one of the best salmon rivers in Scotland, once scribbled an amendment to a Salmon Bill which sought to prevent Canadian salmon being introduced to Scottish rivers. He did so on the back of an envelope in the course of a debate, simply because he happened to know more about the subject than anyone else. "There was no secret about the fact that he owned a salmon river," said his son, "and he declared it. But that didn't mean that the points he was making were any less valid." They were eventually incorporated into the Bill.
>
> (*The Times*, November 3, 1995.)

The presence of interest groups does not so much distort as enhance the House of Lords. For example, the presence of the law lords means that senior representatives of those who will be responsible for interpreting and implementing statutes take part in their drafting, and are able to anticipate difficulties. In practice, the Lords often improve legislation considerably. In the 1994–95 session, for example, they made 228 amendments to the Pensions Bill, 307 to the Environment Bill and 374 to the Children (Scotland) Bill. The Lords also prevailed, against the government's wishes, in matters relating to crime, education, disablement and rural affairs.

There is a partisan element in the Lords which tends to repeat the party line from the Commons, but this co-exists with a more disinterested section of the House. While official government and opposition policies are represented, debate from the red benches is often more wide-ranging and detached than that from the green. It is likely to be more exacting and more scrupulously aimed at achieving a full understanding and a workable result. The Lords, like the civil service of which they are almost a part, can continue with their work without party pettiness, and oblivious to the histrionics of elections.

The case against the Lords is that they do not directly represent the people; but this is also the case for them. They represent the nation in something other than aggregate. They are not sponsored by trade unions or businesses, and their concern is with something larger than the economy. They represent the element of chivalry in national life. And in an age of £1,000-a-plate fundraising dinners and television electioneering, the Lords represent values that, by and large, cannot be bought (although they are prey to the ubiquitous lobbyists). The composition and opinion of their House is not much affected by vulgar party advertising campaigns, which are all about propaganda and have nothing to do with establishing sensible policies. In general, the Lords do not abuse their privilege by putting their personal or collective interests first. On the contrary, they act at least as conscientiously on behalf of the nation as the Commons – not being in thrall to whips – and may be said to be, in Burke's phrase, not an actual but a "*virtual* representation":

> Virtual representation is that in which there is a communion of interests, and a sympathy in feelings and desires between those who act in the name of any description of people, and the people in whose name they act, though the trustees are not actually chosen by them.
>
> (*Letter to Sir Hercules Langrishe.*)

Too few members of the Commons, busy as they are riding their hobby-horses and plotting the advancement of particular causes, obviously cultivate a "sympathy in feelings and desires" with the whole people. But the Lords can, and sometimes do, act impartially on behalf of all sections of the nation, whose interests are thus virtually present in the Upper House.

Allowing monarchs or aristocracies a measure of power is not necessarily antithetical to the wishes of the people. Kings and lords certainly have more grip on the popular imagination than most MPs, and Burke defies the assumption of his critics that those who inherit power must be at odds with the rest of the nation. On the contrary, he argues that just like the Commons they have a responsibility to the whole people, who have lent their authority – their right of self-government – in consenting to be so ruled for their mutual benefit. "The king is the representative of the people; so are the Lords; so are the judges," he wrote in 1770 in *Thoughts on the Present Discontents*. "They are all trustees for the people, as well as the Commons; because no power is given for the sole sake of the holder."

The public acceptance and the useful undemocratic role of the Lords have been repeatedly demonstrated by the many royal commissions and committees of inquiry headed by active peers. Generally, the Lords are considered to be impartial and uncorrupt (and perhaps wiser than elected politicians), and peers are instinctively turned to when governments need advice or adjudication that will be perceived as above party.

Burke could be highly critical about particular hereditary peers, as he was in his withering *Letter to a Noble Lord* of 1796, where he attacked the Duke of Bedford and the Earl of Lauderdale, who were playing at radical politics, unaware that it might destroy them; but he continued to believe in the benefits of a "*natural* aristocracy". He did not suppose that all peers were superior beings. Nonetheless, many did and do strive to live up to their station. With the exception of a few notorious cases, who are tactfully excluded from the House, they behave at least less disgracefully – as far as the newspapers can discover – than the Commons. Again public expectation and indeed peer pressure "points to virtues", to use Burke's expression. Matthew Arnold commented in 1861 on the nobility of an aristocracy already in retreat:

> That elevation of character, that noble way of thinking and behaving, which is an eminent gift of nature to some individuals, is also often generated in whole classes of men (at least when these come of a strong and good race) by the possession of power, by the importance and responsibility of high station, by habitual dealing with great things, by being placed above the necessity of constantly struggling for little things. And it is the source of great virtues. It may go along with a not very quick or open intelligence; but it cannot well go along with a conduct vulgar and ignoble. A governing class imbued with it may not be capable of intelligently leading the masses of a people to the highest pitch of welfare for them; but it sets them an invaluable example of qualities without which no really high welfare can exist.
>
> ("Democracy".)

Heredity cannot guarantee the perpetuation of true nobility, but on the other hand a sense of family honour and public spirit is not unknown. A man who speaks in the Lords as Duke of Wellington or Lord Nelson can command a kind of atavistic respect – at least until he proves himself unworthy. As there can be financial, artistic or musical dynasties – the Bach children, for instance, growing up surrounded by music – so there can be political dynasties (as

William Pitt the Younger knew). The proud idea of dynasty – that children may continue something begun by their parents – is a consolation and encouragement in private life, and it should not lightly be expunged from the realm of government.

The Labour Party wishes to deny the right of hereditary peers to vote. This, however, would make the Upper House a creature of the Lower, as Robert Blake, himself a life peer, has explained:

> Abolition of the hereditary vote . . . is alleged to be phase one of a policy to substitute an elective Upper House for the existing chamber. Meanwhile we would have the biggest quango of all time: a House whose members would owe their seats solely to past or present prime ministerial patronage. Even as an interim measure, this would be thoroughly undesirable, and certainly no improvement on the present composition. The hereditary system, whatever its logical defects, does produce some people of independent opinions and also some who are much younger than the normal run of middle-aged legislators. . . My guess is that after achieving stage one, which would involve a great deal of parliamentary time and much controversy, a Labour Cabinet would rest on its oars and postpone for many years any plans for an elective chamber. There are immense difficulties involved – its powers, electoral system, and above all relations with the Commons, which would certainly resent the creation of a body with rival claims to democratic legitimacy.
>
> (*The Times*, July 23, 1996.)

Sadly, the present feebleness of the Lords stems partly from fear that if the Upper House dissents it will be overruled and humiliated, and partly from the extension of Commons-style party politics into the Lords as its active benches are replenished by former ministers grown grand or senile.

In Burke's age, the royal veto over parliamentary bills had been eroded, but he argues its importance as a kind of reserve power: "The exercise is wisely forborne. Its repose may be the preservation of its existence; and its existence may be the means of saving the constitution itself, on an occasion worthy of bringing it forth." (A wife may promise to love, honour and obey, but the veto of her husband is similarly reserved for emergencies: it had better not be exercised every day.)

Over the past 200 years, the importance of the Lords, too, has been much eroded, but their reserve powers may yet be a means of saving the nation. By Burke's day, the Lords had been excluded for more than a century from control of the nation's finances, which was and is a matter solely for the Commons (because it is from the people that the money comes). So the constitution for which Burke was arguing was far from feudal: power was already most concentrated in the Commons, though not yet exclusively or detrimentally so.

Later the concentration of power became menacing. Since Victorian times, the monarch has not been free without grave consequences to refuse to enact legislation. As Bagehot wrote in 1867, the Queen "must sign her own death-warrant if both Houses unanimously send it up to her". And the Lords too have long been on the defensive. The Upper House now regards itself as a debating, rather than a legislative chamber. Neither has the House of Lords maintained what might have been an important role, as guardian of the constitution. In a mixed government, as an anonymous contemporary of Burke's wrote, there are "more bodies than one possessing not only a nominal, but an actual power of negativing the Acts of each other" ("On Government", Misc MS 697, Pforzheimer Collection, New York). But during the battles over Britain's acceptance of the European Maastricht Treaty in 1993, the Lords failed to prevent the government signing away powers that had been entrusted to it by the people, even though this abrogation was a clear breach of constitutional practice. Clearly this was an example – almost a defining example – of an occasion worthy of bringing forth the Lords' reserve power.

No Parliament can bind future Parliaments, as successive treaties with the EEC, EC and EU have claimed to do. The constitution belongs not to the government but to the nation; it is the property of the people and is not to be wrenched from them by the Commons. "The legislative cannot transfer the power of making laws to any other hands," wrote Locke in his *Second Treatise of Government* (prop. 141; see also prop. 217 and prop. 238). "For it being but a delegated power from the people, they, who have it, cannot pass it over to others." So this handover of power, this usurpation from within is of dubious standing. If it is valid, it is, in Burke's phrase, "iniquitously legal". Tony Benn has described it as "a *coup d'état* by the political class, who didn't believe in popular sovereignty". The first half of this description is exactly right: the government of the day, acting improperly, was not checked by countervailing forces. But Benn's appeal to "popular sovereignty" is exactly wrong: our membership of the Common Market (though never of a political union) was verified by a cowed electorate in a referendum. Democracy ushered in a profoundly undemocratic system. What was missing was not the transitory popular vote, but prudence, a sense of history, effective circumscription of the executive power, the kind of checks that the House of Lords should apply.

It is on the same principle – that the constitution belongs to the nation and not the government – that proposals to deny hereditary peers the right to vote in their own House should be resisted. In this case, the Commons would not be attempting to delegate its powers to foreigners, but attempting to augment its powers at the expense of those who restrain it. Burke, who opposed both George III's attempt to compromise the power of the Commons and later the French revolutionaries' attempt to make all authority democratic, would have been appalled.

Sections of the Commons may wish to abolish the Lords, but neither House should be permitted to meddle in the internal affairs of the other. The independence of the Lords is a protection for us all, both by their practice and by their example. If the Lords' autonomy can simply be overruled, so can that of any other element of the state, or of any other association. The Lords are not part of the elected administration, and should determine to preserve their separate existence. Furthermore, as Burke explained, the Lords' privileges are their property, and are not to be alienated. The peers possess their votes by prescription and heredity, and these are not to be stolen or annulled by another body. In return, the Lords owe us their candid, considered and free opinion, which in these days is potentially more independent than that of the Commons. As the Lower House grows increasingly craven, the independent advice of the Lords to the government becomes ever more valuable. If for the sake of efficiency there is a whipped House, then for the sake of conscience there should also be an unwhipped one.

Abolishing the hereditary principle in the Lords would stealthily increase the pressure for abolition of another undemocratic institution which, if not presently strong, remains popular: the monarchy. No political party yet explicitly challenges the Crown, but its props are being removed (as well as being regularly rammed by young members of the Royal Family at least as reckless as the 18th-century Duke of Bedford and Earl of Lauderdale). Burke explained the threat in a letter of June 1, 1791: "Where all things else are elective, you may call a king hereditary: but he is for the present only a cipher, and all the succession is not supported by any analogy in the state nor combined with any sentiment whatsoever existing in the minds of the people. It is a solitary, unsupported, anomalous thing."

The reforms of 200 years and more have all taken us in the same direction: towards an absolute republican democracy. In that time, no reforms have been proposed, let alone achieved, that would re-form or regroup the contending powers and principles which were once thought so important.

One test of a good constitution is that it be self-limiting, perhaps even self-thwarting. If the constitution is moral and just, Burke wrote, "the body of the commonwealth may remain in all its integrity and be perfectly sound in its composition even if a tyrant or usurper should be at its head". But in its recent dealings with other European nations, the government has not restrained itself at all. Instead it has disregarded the constitution by presuming to bind us to the power of others in perpetuity. If the Commons is thus, like the French Directory, "powerful to usurp, impotent to restore", then the constitutional failure of the other estates is evident. The grammatical apposition Burke uses here was important to him: in the *Reflections* he writes of constitutional arrangements that are "impotent to secure independence, strong only to destroy the rights of men". But such perversions of good government point to the apposition which can ensure a "real *practical* liberty": a government which is (as he re-turned the turn) "powerful to protect, impotent to evade".

13

Checkless and Unbalanced

At the time of the reforms of 1831–32, Coleridge deplored those ministers who had "appealed directly to the argument of the greater number of voices, no matter whether the utterers were drunk or sober, competent or not competent . . . they have done the utmost in their power to raze out the sacred principle in politics of a representation of interests, and to introduce the mad and barbarizing scheme of a delegation of individuals" (*Table Talk*, November 20, 1831). He speaks of the "rights of man" as a "miserable sophism", and says the Reform Act imperils "the triple assent which the constitution requires to the enactment of a valid law" (February 24, 1832). In this he is restating Burke.

For Coleridge, the period 1689–1832 was a constitutional golden age. "The great reform brought into act under William the Third combined the principles truly contended for by Charles [I] and his Parliament respectively; the great revolution of 1831 has certainly, to an almost ruinous degree, dislocated those principles of government again" (May 8, 1833). After the Reform Act, government was carried on, in his eyes, by "a junta of ministers, who were obliged to make common cause with the mob and democratic press for the sake of keeping their places" (February 20, 1833).

Most Whigs hoped that the 1832 Act would be final, a new Act of settlement, but it did not establish a new stability. The progression towards a tyranny of the people by the people had begun. This has since accelerated, as the House of Commons, arguably acting beyond its constitutional competence, and palpably by some chicanes, has stripped the other estates of power. The Lords and monarch now retain only vestigial authority, and are unable to act as correctives, although governments must defer ever more to a fourth estate that lives by exaggeration and exacerbation.

With so little formal counterbalance to the House of Commons, Juvenal's question becomes especially pressing: "Quis custodiet ipsos custodes?" Instead of a moderate balance of powers, public affairs are now run by the Cabinet (which controls the Commons) and by unelected agents such as quangos, bureaucracies and the "regulators" of privatized utilities. As these bodies busy themselves, MPs are free to rabble-rouse, sound-bark and reduce debate to a series of media postures. There is a separation of powers, for sure, but *Quis custodiet quango*?

When the behaviour of some MPs became a visible disgrace early in the 1990s, the House did not discipline itself. Nor was it disciplined by other standing powers. Instead, the Nolan Committee was called to investigate standards in public life. But the notion of a vicarious control upon Parliament logically entails an infinite regress. For if self-regulation by the "honourable Members" is inevitably suspect, then so is regulation. Already questions are being asked about pressures brought to bear upon the regulators. Furthermore, as Enoch Powell observed, deputed regulation not only brings Parliament's integrity and independence into doubt, but positively harms them by removing the assumption of upright behaviour: "We are degrading ourselves by implying that our honour and traditions are not adequate to maintain proper standards in this House." Just as high expectations exert a pressure, so do low ones. And without a presupposition of integrity and trust, no profession can operate, however extensive the regulation may be.

The only alternative to an ultimate power, which is always suspect, is the Burkean solution of mutual restraint, with competing powers in equilibrium or flux and able to hold each other to account. An analogy is professional self-regulation, which operates not by establishing external boards of control, but by allowing different practices to work in harmonious rivalry, each keeping the others up to the mark for fear of the standards and reputation of all being allowed to slip. Membership of a professional body underwrites standards of service to the public, and the threat of expulsion helps to maintain levels of probity. Universities are independent degree-issuing bodies maintaining their own standards, and regulating each other through the use of external examiners. The day their admissions and degrees are subjected to interference from a fabricated panel will mark a defeat for their entire ethos.

Schools, likewise, are best regulated not by national curricula and boards of inspectors, but by subscription to a professional body and by competition for business – by the need to maintain the respect of the profession and the need to prove themselves and attract custom. And just as parents have different scales of values, so schools should play to their various strengths, which might be, say, scientific, sporting, pastoral or musical, and resist the narrowness of judgment by exam results alone.

In Parliament, political parties should be able to regulate each other by insisting on honourable behaviour, while the two Houses each maintain standards in the measures of the other. Yet this mixture of restraint and freedom is no longer working well.

Britain boasts of having "checks and balances" – a dilute Burkeanism – but instead we now have only shreds and patches. And patches on the patches. The call for a new committee to supervise Parliament was an admission that the checks are not working and proclaims that MPs are not to be trusted. Nothing will balance the power of the new commissioner on standards and the standing committee on standards and privileges. The government has apparently put in place a regulator similar to those appointed to oversee the privatized industries, which effectively make arbitrary law and which are answerable to no one. The appallingly named "Ofwat" and "Ofgas" have power to halve or double the profits of huge companies at their whim. Who knows what powers "Ofgov" may expropriate?

By contrast with Burke's organic, time-honoured arrangement of social representation, the "enlightened" doctrine of absolute democracy urges rule solely by the largest number of individuals, and denies the importance of corporate and social stakes in society. People are represented only in the mass, as numbers, and feel little connection with the distant omnipotence that governs. Instead of constituents – those who constitute the body of the nation – they become mere statistics. So are the ligaments of society severed.

As Burke would have expected, the tightening of the rule of majorities alone has brought an ever-increasing clamour from "minorities" who feel themselves systematically excluded. "They reduce men to loose counters merely for the sake of simple telling," Burke complained of the French legislators. And once representation is felt to be a matter solely of numbers, a quota system will not be far behind, with its assumption that only women can represent women, only the blind the blind, only smokers, smokers.

This is precisely the assumption made by Charter 88 when it asserts "MPs cannot properly represent all of us when only one in ten of them are women and only one in a hundred is black". Far from fostering Burke's "communion of interests" and "sympathy in feelings", this kind of assertion is divisive. The logic is that only a 57-year-old Cockney train-driver can represent 57-year-old Cockney train-drivers, and so on, and ultimately that each individual must represent only himself: that we have no mutual or communal interests at all.

The proper role of our representatives was a concern of Burke's. An MP's responsibility is to be well-informed and to bring to Parliament the benefit of his knowledge and experience. He should listen to the concerns of the people, and especially of his constituents, but he always owes them and the country his conscientious opinion.

Burke saw no conflict when he worked as a paid agent for New York whilst an MP. His duty was always first to Parliament, and if his American interests had compromised this, he would have resigned them as a matter of honour. But his aim was to show how the parties to the dispute – the government, the Americans and the British traders – could all gain from reconciliation and from seeing their interests in the round. Understanding of their various needs and fears in such cases helped him to show different groups the whole picture, and how they need not be at odds. (That he was not able to persuade them to give up entrenched positions is another matter.) As an agent, he gained intimate knowledge of American affairs, and he was able to act as a virtual representative. In Parliament he put an American case in which he believed; and to the colonists he explained the mood of Parliament and the benefits of patience. As Frans De Bruyn puts it, "Burke holds out the possibility that interest and disinterest, the public and the private, can be reconciled".

MPs' interests outside the House can clearly benefit Parliament – and might have done so much more in the American case if Burke had been heeded – but they always potentially entail conflicts of loyalty. Either Parliament must do without the benefit, and so legislate over matters on which it is insufficiently informed, or else there must be an official presumption of honour. If the prestige and salary of an MP are high enough, so that he has everything to lose and is properly proud of his situation, and if standards of public behaviour are kept up, then that presumption is possible. But recently the integrity of some MPs, like private moral standards, has fallen so low that there has been an outcry against outside interests. Members have been bought to act as delegates – and not even of their own constituents, but of pressure groups and lobby companies. Now the Nolan report has attempted to end this abuse, but perhaps at the cost of severing professional links which would have enhanced the Commons.

In the early part of Burke's parliamentary career, too, MPs were swayed by interests other than those of the country as a whole. The candour and independence of Members were threatened by George III's attempt to rule by cabal and to circumvent the Commons. So in his *Thoughts on the Present Discontents*, Burke called for parliamentarians to unite against the "King's friends" and to reassert their constitutional role. At a time when shifting alliances had made Parliament unstable and unprincipled, he argued for the longer view, and for coherence. His pamphlet has become the classic statement of the need for political parties:

> It is not enough in a situation of trust in the commonwealth that a man means well to his country; it is not enough that in his single person he never did an evil act, but always voted according to his conscience and even harangued against every design which he apprehended to be prejudicial to the interests of his country. This innoxious and ineffectual character, that seems formed upon a plan of apology and disculpation, falls miserably short of the mark of public duty. That duty demands and requires that what is right should not only be made known, but made prevalent; that what is evil should not only be detected, but defeated.

To this end, men must form connections, agree principles, and learn to act effectively, uniformly and strongly. Parties are "essentially necessary" but "accidentally liable to degenerate into faction". That is, parties fall into evil if they "sink the idea of the general good" in their "circumscribed and partial interest": the common benefit of the commonwealth must always be uppermost.

Burke spelt out the need for political parties to prevent the manipulation of Parliament by the King. But he would also have opposed the manipulation of Parliament by parties. Today parties overwhelmingly dominate politics, and the electorate has an effective choice only between two competing blocks, both of which it may hold in contempt. The choice in the early 1970s, for instance, between an ostensible Conservative who wanted to deliver the country into the hands of foreigners and a socialist who wanted the government to manage the entire economy and to determine incomes and prices was an impossible one for anyone who valued his liberty. And in this last decade of the century, Britain's relations with Europe are of crucial importance, yet the two major parties offer no choice at all, themselves being hopelessly split. "When you've got to choose, Every way you look at it you lose."

Parties in Burke's day were very loose affiliations, and MPs were not dependent upon them. Today they are very tightly controlled, and MPs are pathetically dependent on their high command. The candidates we elect are not our choices but those of the parties, and the candidates' debt to the party managers is constantly called in. "Now the prime responsibility of the member is no longer to his conscience or to the elector, but to his party," wrote Richard Crossman in 1963, in his introduction to Bagehot's *The English Constitution*. "Party loyalty has become the prime political virtue required of an MP, and the test of that loyalty is his willingness to support the official leadership when he knows it to be wrong."

This, to Burke, is "a degree of servitude that no worthy man could bear the thought of submitting to". For an MP should always be his own man. In this matter as in others, Burke argued against apparently opposite dangers. He was scornful both of MPs who were ciphers of the administration and of those who behaved as but messengers from their constituents. Whether they come from the monarch, from the Prime Minister or from the people, "*authoritative* instructions, *mandates* issued, which the member is bound blindly and implicitly to obey, to vote, and to argue for, though contrary to the clearest conviction of his judgment and conscience; – these are things utterly unknown to the laws of this land, and which arise from a fundamental mistake of the whole order and tenor of our constitution" (*Speech to the Electors of Bristol at the Conclusion of the Poll*, 1774).

It was dishonourable for an MP to be anyone's puppet. And this independence and code of honour reduced the importance of the exact method of election or appointment to a position of trust, for however he came into the Commons, an MP's duty was to consider the whole nation. And Burke went further still: "The very inequality of representation, which is so foolishly complained of," he wrote in the *Reflections*, "is perhaps the very thing which prevents us from thinking or acting as Members for districts." This may be going too far, and may be paradoxical, but the aim of loosening the hold of any few people over an MP is a worthy one. If Members of quality and integrity can be brought into Parliament by a variety of means (of which the universal franchise is only one), the nation should gain from their pluralism and diversity. The MP, in Burke's scheme, is not a delegate, he does not wield a block vote or follow a particular mandate, but gives his all in the rightful place of discussion and deliberation: the House of Commons. His job is not to register a predetermined vote, but to discuss, to explain, to listen, to persuade. Parliament, where Burke and others sometimes spoke for hours at a time, presenting properly reasoned and documented arguments, was where political questions were properly decided. Issues were not settled beforehand, elsewhere or in secret, and the chamber was not mainly for show.

Now, however, conscientious independence among MPs is strongly discouraged by the parties, parliamentary debate is reduced to posturing, and oratory has virtually disappeared. On major issues, backbench contributions are limited to ten minutes, so there is little scope for mounting a detailed or concatenated argument. MPs are stooges of their parties, as ministers are agents of the Prime Minister. Backbenchers can hardly hope to influence events by force of argument, and instead descend into the parroting of party propaganda and the asking of fawning, rhetorical questions of ministers. They are present in the Commons under false pretences: from their own point of view as trainee ministers, and from the parties' point of view as a numerical necessity. All must be prepared to acquiesce in legislation that they know to be wrong, for they have no independent standing. Burke wrote in 1770 that "an indiscriminate support of all administrations [had] totally banished all integrity and confidence out of public proceedings". But as Crossman observed, it was the old independence of the private member which "gave the Commons its collective character and made it the most important check on the executive". Without this, more and more power is concentrated in fewer and fewer hands – which is quite the opposite of what people suppose when they mouth the term "democracy". Except that the Prime Minister, rather than the King, now controls the ministers, the danger is comparable to that described by Burke in the "Representation to His Majesty" of June 14, 1784:

> A House of Commons respected by his ministers is essential to His Majesty's service: it is fit that [the ministers] should yield to Parliament, and not that Parliament should be new modelled until it is fitted to their purposes. If our authority is only to be held up when we coincide in opinion with His Majesty's advisers, but is to be set at nought the moment it differs from them, the House of Commons will sink into a mere appendage of administration; and will lose that independent character which, inseparably connecting the honour and reputation with the acts of this House, enables us to afford a real, effective, and substantial support to his government.

Without the restraint of an independent Commons, ministers often behave as though they were the masters of the people, rather than their servants. To a small degree, the monarchy still reminds them that they are temporary and answerable appointees – at the Prime Minister's weekly meeting with the Queen it is the politician who is granted an audience and the monarch who obviously represents the whole national interest, from outside politics – but this barely amounts to a restraint.

The Crown, the Lords and the Commons scarcely restrain the executive, so parliamentary power has been concentrated in the hands of the Prime Minister and Cabinet. In the 19th century, Bagehot, who understood the strength of the Cabinet, suggested that the House of Commons and the Prime Minister were checks upon one another because each could dismiss the other, but this threat of mutual destruction is too final to be a day-to-day deterrent. Instead, we have what Lord Hailsham has described as "elective dictatorship".

A Prime Minister may have the support of less than 50 per cent of the people; or of votes cast; or even of seats in the Commons. (Not since the general election of 1935 has the ruling party won a true majority of the votes cast.) Yet the Prime Minister appoints and directs his Cabinet, and can whip his party to support almost any policy, so controlling the House. What is thus passed by the Commons cannot practicably be resisted anywhere else, so we have a small body "with every possible power, and no possible external control" – as Burke described the French National Assembly of 1790, again deploying his favourite grammatical apposition. A small and powerful cabal made up mostly of men of similar ages and backgrounds (the Cabinet) is able to pass laws which benefit the part of the nation that it represents, without regard to harm that may be done to those in quite different situations. Believing that it has a mandate, this cabal is liable to triumphalism and to indifference towards other interests which have been "defeated".

The supposed "majority" may be smaller than the sum of the several minorities that have been outvoted, and yet a parliamentary majority confers a narrow, divisive power, rather than encouraging those in power to represent *all* the people. A sectional purpose and a partial will are mistaken for the whole, and the cabal is liable to forget the vital freedom of minorities not to be imposed upon by parliamentary or other majorities. But people's needs and concerns are not identical, and Parliament cannot rule on behalf of all by ignoring differences and trying to assimilate every contending interest to its own. "A forced and fictitious agreement (which every universal agreement must be)," wrote Burke in a letter on April 12, 1780, "is not becoming the cause of freedom."

If anything, the overwhelming of minority interests by the Cabinet is worse than other forms of sectarian rule, for the granting of equal votes has disguised the disgrace that those who vote for unsuccessful parties are not meaningfully represented at all in a democracy. "The beaten party", Burke writes,

> are exasperated and soured by the previous contention, and mortified by the conclusive defeat. This mode of decision, where wills may be so nearly equal, where, according to circumstances, the smaller number may be the stronger force, and where apparent reason may be all upon one side, and on the other little else than impetuous appetite; all this must be the result of a very particular and special convention. . .
>
> (*Appeal to the Old Whigs.*)

In this sense, democracy may be less representative and inclusive than aristocracy.

So with democracy as its G-string of decency, Britain now has a narrow, divisive autocracy amounting to arbitrary rule for as long as a Commons majority holds. Its supposedly popular government is unpopular most of the time, among a people who have little control over it and rarely feel that they have entrusted power to a body that properly represents them. Nor yet do they feel they are led by men and women of distinction and superior merit, for the leaders themselves decry the very idea. Parliament is felt to be an extrinsic agency, accountable more or less to the spin of a wheel once in five years. As Burke feared in his *Reflections*, democracy has an "inevitable tendency to party tyranny". This is government neither by consent nor by consensus, for millions feel excluded from the constitution which is their birthright. Suspicion has taken the place of consent. And ever-increasing doses of democracy, labelled as a panacea but prescribed as a sedative, are making matters worse.

Even Burke has little to say about how to regain the people's consent if it is once lost. In his *Speech on Fox's East India Bill*, he argues that all political power is a trust – "and it is of the very essence of every trust to be rendered *accountable*; and even totally to *cease*, when it substantially varies from the purposes for which alone it could have a lawful existence." Parliament should consider this carefully and constantly.

14

A People Proud and Great

For most of this century, Britain has been retreating from its old complacent idea of its own destiny. Ours has become an apologetic, uncertain, cynical culture.

The callous commanders of the First World War shattered the comforting belief that the governing class was competent and trustworthy, and in its place arose a belief that it was merely self-serving. Subsequently, the end of empire dented British self-esteem and brought an exaggerated sense of guilt. It came to be believed that all colonies, settlements or administrations were deliberate, systematic oppression of the natives, and that the British Empire had been the worst because it was the largest. But of the colonizers, the British had been in general perhaps the most fastidious. In a letter of 1773, Johnson wrote: "I do not much wish well to discoveries, for I am always afraid that they will end in conquest and robbery." Sometimes, as in India, they did, but the British deserve a modicum of credit for having curbed their own excesses. Burke's own disinterested campaign against the massive oppression in India helped to set at least some limits to private exploitations. Slavery was abolished not by uprisings, but by the triumph of humanity. By the Victorian era, the empire spirit included considerable elements of duty, responsibility and altruism. This attitude is now routinely ridiculed, but it embodied an honourable code that has not been superseded.

When Britain granted independence to the colonies, it was on principles akin to those that Burke propounded in our dealings with America. Instead of fighting and losing further wars of independence, Britain acknowledged native aspirations. In some cases the British withdrew too abruptly, but the end of empire was mostly managed with grace, and relations with many former colonies are amicable.

Yet the sapping of British self-belief and self-reliance continued. As Margaret Thatcher has said, "The two great wars of this century whetted government's appetite for increased spending. Politicians became used to wielding tremendous power, and ordinary people to accepting it." After the crippling effort of the Second World War, when Churchill had stubbornly resisted an evil against all reasonable odds, Britain's stamina was exhausted. With the best of intentions, the wartime command economy was translated into the welfare state; but whereas obedience to the grand plan is essential in war to achieve the single overwhelming objective, centralization and passivity are not appropriate to the multiple purposes and pursuits of peace. Economically, Britain began to fall behind other nations (not least Germany and Japan, which were forbidden to rearm, and so avoided that wasteful drain on resources). Genteel decay was thought to be inevitable in Britain – "The business of the civil service is the orderly management of decline," said its top man in 1973 – and many people gave up the struggle to achieve the highest standards. A lazy attitude spread: that there was safety in mediocrity and that second-best was best.

Intellectuals concocted an egalitarian ideology to cover this retreat and to justify anti-élitism. More and more emphasis was put on questions of race, but pride in Britain's achievements was treated as distasteful. So those who should have been cultural leaders became reluctant to celebrate its successes and to acclaim the extraordinarily creative, scientific and civilizing history of the British. Instead, as Norman Stone has said, history is taught to children as "a series of grievances". In Britain, now, every race can hold its head up except the English. A well-founded confidence was undermined and mocked. Yet there is still a strong case that Great Britain has been the most remarkable nation of all. Certainly our achievements compare with those of ancient Greece or Renaissance Italy.

It is more than 200 years since Burke, as a Whig historian, wrote of "the happy experience of this country of a growing liberty and a growing prosperity for five hundred years". Since then Britain has repeatedly stood up for liberty in the world, and has continued to grow more prosperous. So we may now, without too much exaggeration, boast of *seven* centuries of a growing liberty and a growing prosperity.

England, as John Bright said, is the mother of parliaments and Britain has perhaps the longest record of liberal government of any country. British justice has an exemplary record of principled, pragmatic fairness, and has until recently remained immune to attempts at political interference. Britain has given the world its universal language, incomparably its greatest literature, and its greatest writer. British scientists have led the world, from Newton to Darwin, to the splitting of the atom and the unravelling of DNA. British science was quick to organize itself through the Royal Society, and British art did the same through the Royal Academy. Similar bodies have promoted other branches of learning, and the British accordingly laid the foundations of disciplines from economics to hydrostatics. Britain has two of the great universities of the world, some of the greatest libraries and museums, the greatest academic publisher, and the world's most famous – and probably best – schools (though now also some of the worst).

British theatre is among the most varied and inventive in the world. There is more classical music in London than anywhere else, and the Proms are the world's largest music festival. The greatest pop group and the greatest rock band have both been British. The country has some 250 theatres, 2,500 museums and public galleries, 200 orchestras, 70 dance companies and 4,000 public libraries.

British explorers have been some of the most intrepid, from the conquering of new worlds to the scaling of Everest. The British armed forces are among the most effective (not least because of their loyalty to their little platoons). The British invented almost all of the major sports now enjoyed worldwide, and Britain is still the headquarters of many of them. The world's two leading auctioneers both have their roots in Britain. The City of London is one of the financial centres of the world, and Britain remains a great trading nation. Thanks to its inventors, Britain was the first nation to industrialize. Britain pioneered railways, iron ships and iron bridges, photography, telephony, radio and television broadcasting, and computing. Britain has a world-class record in painting, music, architecture, fashion, television and newspapers. In our harsh century, just as during the French Revolution, the country has been hospitable to innumerable refugees and émigrés, among whom have been remarkable numbers of artists, writers, philosophers, historians and other intellectuals. Freud, Wittgenstein, Eliot, Gombrich, Popper and Hayek are among those who have elected to call these islands home. British life and lives are diverse and resistant to regimentation. We may justly think of British achievements as Burke thought of France's in his *Reflections*: "when I survey the state of all the arts that beautify and polish life; when I reckon the men she has bred for extending her fame in war, her able statesmen, the multitude of her profound lawyers and theologians, her philosophers, her critics, her historians and antiquaries, her poets and her orators sacred and profane, I behold in all this something which awes and commands the imagination". Great Britain's is not a record about which we need feel defensive. But if we are again to give the world a lead, we must recover our belief in what Burke referred to as "that salutary prejudice called our country".

Britain has nothing to fear but self-doubt. The post-war timidity has been exemplified by our attitude to the Common Market and its successor, the European Union. Most British people are instinctively loath to surrender into the hands of a foreign coalition an independent nation that has not been conquered since 1066; and yet for 30 years politicians have warned us of our inadequacy. We have been told that we cannot survive alone, that if we do not influence the European Union it will exclude us, refuse to trade with us, and leave us exposed in the world. The EU has taken our money and then given us back a fraction, at which the credulous have exclaimed that without such handouts we would face penury. And the people have lacked the confidence to call the bluff or the means to express their will. It has been unfashionable to proclaim that Great Britain is not like the rest of Europe, but is a special case, both because we are an island and because we are a special people. So gradually our freedoms have been given away, and the national property has been turned over to others. We have signed treaty after treaty not because we believe in them, or even understand them, but because we have been afraid of the imaginary consequences of refusing. We have not been bribed into Europe – for what has it to offer us? – but blackmailed. "That England, that was wont to conquer others, Hath made a shameful conquest of itself."

The British are slow to be roused. We like to believe the best of others, to appease rather than to confront. Rather than admit that we are being exploited, we choose to ignore the evidence. Accordingly, British politicians have for year after year, decade after decade, told themselves and the public that next time we will prevail in

European negotiations, that another conference will persuade the French and the Germans; that with just one more compromise the train or the boat or the window of opportunity or the level playing field or the "variable geometry" – God help us – or some other nonsense will start to favour us. We have been told that the EU's stated, agreed and signed aim of "ever-closer union" means a loose trading arrangement. We have been told that we are succeeding or will one day succeed in changing the unifying ambitions of the other nations.

Our negotiations with the EU have uncannily paralleled Britain's dealings with post-revolutionary France. We have been pusillanimous where we ought to be bold, craven where we ought to be proud. "They must be worse than blind who do not see with what undeviating regularity of system, in this case and in all cases, they pursue their scheme for the utter destruction of every independent power," wrote Burke in 1796 in his *Letters on a Regicide Peace.*

France had declared war on Britain in February 1793, and Burke argued that the French Directory was not prepared to compromise, but was by its own logic uncompromising. Its pretensions, like those of Brussels today, were non-negotiable, so it was better not to negotiate. "On the head of what is *not* to be the subject of negotiation, the Directory is clear and open. As to what may be a matter of treaty, all this open dealing is gone. She retires into her shell. There she expects overtures from *you* – and that you are to guess what she shall judge just, reasonable, and above all, *compatible with her dignity.*" The mandarins of the European Union have similarly limited what may be discussed or renegotiated at inter-governmental conferences. The conclusions are already agreed. All we can do is meekly give the reply expected of us. As the Danes discovered, if the people come up with the wrong answer in a referendum, they will be asked again until they give the right one. This is Soviet-style vote-rigging.

Burke judged the "Regicide Directory" by its record. Its interests had always proved to be at odds with those of a free Britain, and so, he thought, they were likely always to prove in future. British fishermen and beef farmers might see a parallel today. In 25 years of membership, British interests have never yet prevailed in the councils of Europe. We have attended a long series of conferences, proclaiming that we will not surrender this, that and the other element of our freedom, only to be told that we have no choice, that the matter falls under some previous treaty, and that we have no veto. Time after time, our firm stands have turned to capitulation. "We will not give way. We will not give way. We will not . . . oh, all right then." The government argues that we must take part, so that we can influence events. Yet again and again we have taken part only to be ignored. Our "partners" can scarcely disguise their contempt as they mulct us. The glee and alacrity with which the EU over-reacted to fears of BSE in cattle show how little has changed. Not only did the other member countries refuse to import our beef themselves, but they banned Britain from exporting to non-members – so claiming the right to regulate our trade with the entire world. So we are to be a subject people. Burke found this attitude intolerable:

> In other words, their will is the law, not only at home, but as to the concerns of every nation. Who has made that law but the Regicide Republic itself, whose laws, like those of the Medes and Persians, they cannot alter or abrogate, or even so much as take into consideration. Without the least ceremony or compliment, they have sent out of the world whole sets of laws and lawgivers. They have swept away the very constitutions under which the legislatures acted, and the laws were made . . . whatever they have put their seal on for the purposes of their ambition, and the ruin of their neighbours, this alone is invulnerable, impassible, immortal. . . In other words, they are powerful to usurp, impotent to restore; and equally by their power and their impotence they aggrandize themselves, and weaken and impoverish you and all other nations.
>
> (*Letters on a Regicide Peace.*)

British ministers attempting to negotiate a lifting of the beef export ban found the EU behaving with all the contempt and hauteur of the revolutionary French, as Burke described them: "Every demonstration of an implacable rancour and an untameable pride were the only encouragements we received to the renewal of our supplications."

Like the Commission today, the Directory of 1796 believed that it had not just a right but a duty to impose its laws upon Europe. It insisted that, "charged by the Constitution with the execution of the *laws*, it cannot *make* or *listen* to any proposal that would be contrary to them. The Constitutional Act does not permit it to consent to any alienation of that which, according to the existing laws, constitutes the territory of the Republic". Equally today, the European Courts must be the final arbiters. And the basis of these laws is precisely the kind of abstraction that was propounded during the French Revolution. The European Court of Human Rights is the direct descendant of the "rights of man", which claimed a universal jurisdiction.

Like some backbenchers, whom the party leaders deride, Burke was incensed by this attitude in Europe. "It is insolent in words, in manner, but in substance it is not only insulting but alarming. It is a specimen of what may be expected from the masters we are preparing for our humbled country. Their openness and candour consist in a direct avowal of their despotism and ambition." In entering negotiations yet again with the EU – as with France two centuries ago – we cannot say we were tricked: "they have informed you of the result they propose . . . to grant you; that is to say, the union they propose among nations with the view of rivalling our trade and destroying our naval power. . . They make no scruple beforehand to tell you the whole of what they intend. . ." A superstate run by Germany and administered from Brussels is what they intend. Protectionism, a single currency, bureaucracy in place of private enterprise, uniformity, obedience, intrusion in every facet of commercial life, the removal of national institutions. That is what they intend.

Burke goes on to argue that "under the auspices of this declaration, we cannot, with the least hope of a good event, or, indeed, with any regard to the common safety, proceed in the train of this negotiation" – because to do so is tantamount to accepting the proffered terms.

> If humiliation is the element in which we live, if it is become not only our occasional policy but our habit, no great objection can be made to the modes in which it may be diversified. . . But to send a gentleman there on no other errand than this, and with no assurance whatever that he should not find, what he did find, a repulse, seems to me to go far beyond all the demands of a humiliation merely politic. I hope it did not arise from a predilection for that mode of conduct.

Does Britain, from misplaced shame about its past power, now enjoy abasing itself?

Our delegations to future conferences should be sure of their reserve power. They should have authority to veto the negotiations entirely, for we have heard what the other nations intend to impose upon us. "Whoever goes to the directorial presence under this passport, with this offensive comment, and foul explanation, goes, in the avowed sense of the court to which he is sent; as the instrument of a government dissociated from the interests and wishes of the nation. . . He has national weakness for his full powers . . . it would be pleasant to read his instructions on the answer which he is to give to the Directory, in case they should repeat to him the substance of the manifesto. . ."

We are fighting for survival as a nation. "The question is not now how we are to be affected with it in regard to our dignity. That is gone. I shall say no more about it. Light lie the earth on the ashes of English pride." However, British politicians still countenance yet further usurpations of national and parliamentary powers, such as control over our money. "If this be our deliberate mind, truly we deserve to lose, what it is impossible we should long retain, the name of a nation." As Burke wrote on the first page of the *Letters on a Regicide Peace*: "To a people who have once been proud and great, and great because they were proud, a change in the national spirit is the most terrible of all revolutions."

The great change in the national spirit is perhaps that people no longer feel they are ruled by consent. Explaining why Burke would have opposed the Maastricht Treaty, his biographer Conor Cruise O'Brien wrote: "The Prime Minister and the leaders of the Opposition are determined to push the British people into a [federalist] project that they know the people would reject if they were allowed a say in the matter" (*The Times*, February 20, 1993). All party leaders weakly say that we need not make up our minds yet about the European Union's future, as if we had not. We should wait to hear all the arguments, they say, as though these could ever end. But the movement of the ratchet is quite apparent, and the people know what is happening. They feel powerless and demoralized because Britain does not want to be part of what is going to happen. Over the single currency, for instance, politicians tell us we must "wait and see"; but as Burke wrote, "the counsels of pusillanimity very rarely put off, whilst they are always sure to aggravate, the evils from which they would fly."

He also predicted what has not yet happened – that if Britain subordinates itself to another power, the people will eventually find that even their internal leaders are chosen for them: "If we once place ourselves in a state of inferiority", he wrote in a letter of March 1, 1797, "they will now, and at all times, in effect, name a [prime] minister to this country. There never has been a superior power who would suffer a dependent province substantially to name its own minister." It may be that the European Union will continue to allow Britain to choose figurehead Prime Ministers, but it is likely that it will try to "harmonize" the domestic legislative arrangements of its member states. It is possible that a directive from a European court will eventually rule that Britain may not have a monarchy, and may not have an unelected Upper House, on the grounds that these are not democratic (and it is unlikely to be receptive to the argument that this is their point). We may expect to be told that we must conform to someone else's abstract idea of what makes a good constitution. It would be peculiar if we were made to conform in litres and metres, in fridges and bridges, without there being an eventual intention to standardize and homogenize our parliamentary system too. That Britain's record of free government is matched by none of the major continental powers which threaten to impose upon us only makes this more likely. Who the hell do these British think they are?

Burke's description of the French Assembly is astonishingly appropriate to the gradual usurpations of what began as a coal and steel confederation and now dictates to governments and to peoples:

> I can never consider this assembly as anything else than a voluntary association of men, who have availed themselves of circumstances to seize upon the power of the state. They have not the sanction and authority of the character under which they first met. They have assumed another of a very different nature; and have completely altered and inverted all the relations in which they originally stood. They do not hold the authority they exercise under any constitutional law of the state. They have departed from the instructions of the people by whom they were sent; which instructions, as the assembly did not act in virtue of any ancient usage or settled law, were the sole source of their authority. The most considerable of their acts have not been done by great majorities. . .
>
> (*Reflections*.)

David Pryce-Jones has written that the European Union is "an act of pure will on the part of a very limited number of politicians", and that "whether or not they wish for it, whole populations are once again to be improved in the name of centralization and modernization". Absence of consent, he continues, "introduces confusion and conflict, even an ultimate prospect of armed enforcement or collapse, in an uncanny Western echo of the Soviet experiment." But behind the Soviet experiment stands the great archetype of the Jacobin revolution.

Although he did not live to see Napoleon's rise, Burke rightly predicted that the coercive European union of his day would become a dictatorship that would have to be fought. The Directory claimed sovereignty over the very things that the European Union is now presuming to control: industry, agriculture, the sea, money.

> The design is wicked, immoral, impious, oppressive; but it is spirited and daring; it is systematic; it is simple in its principle; it has unity and consistency in perfection. In that country entirely to cut off a branch of commerce, to extinguish a manufacture, to destroy the circulation of money, to violate credit, to suspend the course of agriculture, even to burn a city, or to lay waste a province of their own, does not cost them a moment's anxiety. To them, the will, the wish, the want, the liberty, the toil, the blood of individuals is as nothing. Individuality is left out of their scheme of government. The state is all in all.

Burke had foreseen the very essence of totalitarianism. And what did he conclude? "From all this, what is my inference? It is, that this new system of robbery in France, cannot be rendered safe by any art; that it *must* be destroyed, or that it will destroy all Europe."

15

Presuming upon the Future

Dr Johnson warned: "Things modified by human understandings, subject to varieties of complication, and changeable as experience advances knowledge or accident influences caprice, are scarcely to be included in any standing form of expression, because they are always suffering some alteration of their state" (*Rambler* No 125).

That most British of virtues, cricket, retains in its laws an appeal to gentlemanly conduct: "42.1 The captains are responsible at all times for ensuring that play is conducted within the spirit of the game as well as within the Laws. 42.2 The umpires are the sole judges of fair and unfair play." These are exemplary rules. The first appeals to something beyond mere rules – the *spirit* of the game – and so avows that standing forms of expression are never enough; and the second affirms the full authority of those in a position to adjudicate best: on the ground. The very word "umpire" has about it something conciliatory, rather than legalistic, which is exactly caught in Johnson's definition: "one who, as a common friend, decides disputes". Consent is better than enforcement. Happy the well-disciplined school where the only rule is that pupils shall behave properly, and where they are thought-provokingly told "You are here to bring honour to this school", and left to determine for themselves how to fulfil this duty. The aim is not a regulated conformity, but the beginnings of responsible citizenship.

Written constitutions pretend to know better, and to judge before every event. This is a pernicious, because inflexible, form of prejudging: presumption. But despite their pretence of finality, written constitutions are liable to accrue ever more technical amendments as changing circumstances and technologies make their limitations plain. So instead of being statements of broad principle, they tend to decline into cumbersome charters of law which are especially rigid because supposedly above politics.

"Constitution" means the nature of things. The human constitution is what cannot be changed, or can be changed only with the utmost difficulty over a long period. A national constitution is the same: it should describe how things work, not try to determine them. The phrase "the British constitution" can mean either the character of John Bull (which has to do with roast beef and hearts of oak) or the arrangements of his politics, and as the phrase tells us, the two naturally coincide. To constitute is, in Johnson's pleasing tautology, "to make anything what it is", not to make it something else. The constitution acknowledges the existing and permanent make-up of a people and a country. Yet the calls of Charter 88, for instance, are not for consolidation but for innovation: "We should have a written constitution, to set out the new relationship between us and the state". Not to constitute, then, but to re-constitute; not to make us what we are, but to make us something new.

There may be times when it is necessary to write a new constitution or code of laws, but this, as Burke says, is likely to be after a national cataclysm, such as defeat in war or a declaration of independence. Then the task will be hard enough. But to write a new constitution for a country that is living consensually by longstanding arrangements is harder yet, and an invitation to controversy and bitterness. It is to declare an emergency when there is none.

The oldest national written constitution still in use, that of the United States, had the advantage of being framed by sagacious leaders establishing a nation. But noble though it is, the American Constitution has undergone periodic revision and reversion. For example, the constitutional amendment prohibiting alcohol, introduced in 1919, had to be repealed in 1933. This was not truly a constitutional matter, but a law.

The American Constitution has also become a battlefield for conflicts over which rights shall prevail. It takes power away from the government and gives it to judges, who necessarily become politicized. For instance, the states have seen their power to impose the death penalty first arbitrarily abolished and then arbitrarily restored by the Supreme Court as a constitutional question, without Congress having a vote on it at all.

To define our inheritance of British liberties under a charter or bill of rights or written constitution would be to confine them. Yet at the same time, if the American experience is any indication, such a document would require an interpretative court and would not be a permanent apolitical fixture, but a recurrent political fix. Even more than that of the United States, a constitution written now would be couched in the too-specific, too-narrow and yet indefinitely extendable terms of human rights, rather than as an appeal to fairness with the spirit of the laws entrusted to benign legislators and umpires. It would be based not upon wisdom and experience, but upon a grand philosophical confusion.

"All your sophisters cannot produce anything better adapted to preserve a rational and manly freedom than the course that we have pursued, who have chosen our nature rather than our speculations, our breasts rather than our inventions, for the great conservatories and magazines of our rights and privileges," wrote Burke in the *Reflections*. He was right. As sophistry and speculation have encroached – for instance since Britain agreed to be bound by the European Court of Human Rights – the sense of justice and liberty that springs in our breasts has retreated. All too many people are ready to accept with a shrug rulings that they feel are unjust or regulations they feel are unwarranted, simply because the sophisters say they have no choice.

Britain's constitution has historically been based on a spirit of compromise. Our jurisprudence relies heavily on precedent, yet no judgment is binding on cases in the future, when circumstances may have altered. The present and future are bound to the past, but not by it. A written constitution for these islands could not improve upon these arrangements, which have long prevented arbitrary government. Ministers cannot rule by despotic caprice, but must act within the rule of law. Judges can and do tell ministers if they are exceeding their powers, although ministers can change the law with the assent (now too readily granted) of the necessary parliamentary majorities.

Today, however, Britain is subject to arbitrary diktats – from abroad. No written British constitution will put a stop to these, because the European Union claims to have powers transcending those of nations, and to be subject solely to the judgments of its own courts. Only by rejecting these external powers altogether can Britain regain its constitutional equilibrium. And because that equilibrium is not a fixed thing but a continual balancing of contending powers and interests, it cannot be set down in final form. Not surprisingly, many of those who would bind us under a written constitution would bind us also to the provisions of the European monolith, for they believe not in the dispersal and separation of powers, but in a concentrated, central authority.

The idea that introducing a written constitution for the United Kingdom would put an end to constitutional wrangling is naïve and incredible. To begin with, any constitution compiled at present would not be freely entered into by a free people, because it would be constrained by our supposed obligations to other countries in Europe. The writers of a constitution would not, for instance, feel able to determine the nature of the highest court of appeal, or the autonomy of Parliament. These are currently under the control of powers beyond the nation, though this is widely resented, and such limitations would make it impossible to compose a free constitution.

A few years ago, the newly appointed editor of a national newspaper made the mistake of throwing away a house style-guide that had been compiled over decades, and writing his own. He issued directions on matters that scarcely arose, while omitting to rule on genuinely crucial points. Nor could he know the reasons – of consistency, literary convention or legal propriety – why successive sub-editors had adopted and passed on particular practices. He looked for system, and did not find it; what he overlooked was a series of working methods. The newspaper had not been publishing since the age of Edmund Burke without considering stylistic issues. The paper's previous style notes had been compiled and adjusted in response to circumstances; the new guide was written all at once and imposed (aptly enough in the form of a little red book). It did not work, and had swiftly to be rewritten. What had previously been second nature had been so much investigated and discussed that the paper had become self-conscious, and in some cases pedantic and unidiomatic.

To attempt to write a constitution from scratch would be to make the same mistake. For like the style-book, Britain's unwritten constitution is, in Burke's phrase, "the result of the thoughts of many minds, in many ages". And of course the style-book of a newspaper is a trivial thing by comparison with a constitution. If the serviceable elegance of such a painstakingly compiled *vade mecum* was not apparent to the reformer, the moral and practical dimensions of an ancient constitution are not likely to be apparent either. And how much greater would be the consequences of misunderstanding them.

The inevitable disputes over the writing of a new constitution would signal that the whole system was contingent and subject to revision. This would be a grave concession to meddlers who, in Burke's words, "think they have no liberty, if it does not comprehend a right in them of making to themselves new constitutions at their pleasure". Thus while the form of words would have to be rigid and obstinate, the political pressure for alterations to suit passing fancies would be enormous. A constitution intended to settle matters would itself become a grievance – "a subject", as Burke wrote in the *Reflections*, "rather of altercation than enjoyment".

Nations resort to written constitutions when ill at ease. A nation constantly referring to one is akin to a couple continually discussing the state of their relationship instead of living it. Nation and relationship are both liable to be made unhappy and less stable by worrying away unnecessarily at matters that might never arise in practice.

The analogy has been taken farthest by a couple from – obviously – the United States, who drew up for themselves a marital constitution, which lays out what are to be their life aims, their separate responsibilities, how often they are to have sex and when they shall have children. Well, by his fifties Tristram Shandy's father had come to regulate married life so that he wound the house-clock on the first Sunday night of every month, and "had likewise gradually brought some other little family concernments to the same period, in order, as he would often say to my uncle *Toby*, to get them all out of the way at one time" – but this was in fiction. One can only pity a couple so lacking in spontaneity that they must regulate their sexual lives like clockwork. They are dreaming of a system so perfect that they will not have to feel sexy. By living to an agenda they hope to overcome their absence of imagination, tolerance, flexibility and trust. Doubtless the divorce will be for breach of contract.

Burke is right to argue that a contented society (like a contented relationship) does not crave theoretical underpinnings. "The bulk of mankind on their part are not excessively curious concerning any theories whilst they are really happy; and one sure symptom of an ill-conducted state is the propensity of the people to resort to them." Such questions are raised only when a tacit faith is violated, as America's independence began to be demanded only when Parliament began to tax the colonies: "The same cause which has introduced all formal compacts and covenants among men made it necessary. I mean habits of soreness, jealousy, and distrust." A written constitution is not a victory, but an admission of defeat, of soreness, jealousy and distrust. Just as people's wishes and needs should be addressed directly, rather than escalated into abstract questions of "rights", so political problems should not be escalated into "constitutional issues" if this can possibly be avoided.

One of the evils of our involvement with the European Union is that Britain has been for decades constantly "in negotiation" over the technicalities of one treaty after another. The treaties of Vienna and Versailles may have been difficult and rancorous, but they aimed at least to agree a settlement. In the European Union, nothing is ever settled, nor meant to be. Everything is provisional, part of the great historic progress, and our constitution is under threat day after day, year after year.

The political commentator Peter Riddell has acutely observed that a written constitution is being imposed upon Britain by stealth, in the form of ever-tighter rules and procedures for ministers, MPs, government bureaux and the civil service. Instead of placing our trust in the integrity of our governors, we are asked to rely on a jumble of technicalities – just as justice is now supposed to be secured not by the integrity of the courts, but by endless legal safeguards. And yet no exactness can satisfy these hopes. The new rules may be welcomed by the thoughtless, because they promise to punish particular breaches, but they will be deplored by the reflective, because once again they suggest that all behaviour that is not proscribed is acceptable, and that MPs, ministers and civil servants need use not their judgment, but their wiles only. As Burke once observed, rigour tends to defeat itself. These formal compacts are yet another victory for distrust – which they will not banish but promote.

16

Tradition

Most people know how to conduct themselves without a rulebook. They know how to behave because they have grown up behaving within the bounds of a tradition. It is through the complexities of tradition and a multiplicity of institutions that a regulated society is compatible with liberty.

Tradition is often stigmatized. As T. S. Eliot pointed out in 1917, writing about literary tradition, it is erroneously considered by many people to be either stultifying or merely archaeological, "whereas if we approach a poet without this prejudice we shall often find that not only the best, but the most individual parts of his work may be those in which the dead poets, his ancestors, assert their immortality most vigorously" ("Tradition and the Individual Talent"). In politics, as in literature and family life, tradition is inescapable. We do not build from nothing, but we can transform what we are taught, and transmit what we add or discover.

Just as Burke tried to explain to the uncomprehending Thomas Paine that institutions are not constraints upon liberty but its medium, so Eliot argued in the same terms about tradition. And the modern philosopher Michael Oakeshott, aptly liberated by the thoughts of Burke and Eliot, took the story a little further in his own terms. In his book on Oakeshott, Robert Grant summarizes:

> Though not in any foreseeable manner, [tradition] is always evolving . . . because . . . the individual is never a mere passive receptacle of tradition (as he might be of merely technical knowledge). He is not mechanically "determined" by it, for it is transformed and extended by his own personal contribution. Indeed, without tradition, the individual would have (as with a language) no terms in which to express himself.
>
> A tradition, then, is not so much (as the radical or "progressive" would have it) a constraint on individuality, as its precondition. To empty the mind of its environmental filling – that is, of its practical knowledge, or what Burke defiantly called its "prejudice" – in pursuit of an allegedly enhanced "rationality" is in fact to empty it of everything that makes it a mind.

To clear your mind of cant, as Dr Johnson advised, is one thing, but to clear your mind of everything you ever knew in order to think more clearly – as 18th-century rationalists aspired to do – is quite another. Burke defined Jacobinism as an attempt "to eradicate prejudice out of the minds of men". Doing so does not help people to think, though it may make them easier to control.

Traditions, however, are not immutable. Languages are good examples of living traditions. What we learn (and to an extent are perhaps born with) is a basic pattern, a resource that enables us to think and to articulate for ourselves. Every generation modifies the language and yet hands on something continuous with what went before. We can understand our forefathers, but we do not speak quite as they did. On the other hand, many people are properly suspicious of attempts to shift the language abruptly for political purposes, as when we are told our usage is "sexist". Distorting language as a form of social control does not liberate it or us, but is characteristic of intolerant and utopian regimes. The French revolutionaries attempted to impose their own terminology; so did the communist revolutionaries. Orwell writes of the coercive, numbing effect of these jargons when he describes Newspeak, a language that is engineered rather than traditional and spontaneous.

Like language, moral and social conventions have semi-autonomous lives. They are organic – growing, shedding skins, but maintaining an identity. Traditions too are forms of growth. They too can die. After death they may be academically decoded, but they can never be revived.

A great culture can as surely be allowed to die – or abandoned to the archaeologists – as a great literature. Yet the human make-up does not change, so although there are dark ages, some of what is destroyed will be restored in a new form. Freud pointed out, for instance, that the importance of dreams in our psychology was recognized by the ancients, only to be dismissed, and then rediscovered at the end of the 19th century.

As Eliot wrote in *East Coker*:

> There is only the fight to recover what has been lost
> And found and lost again and again...

Because human needs do not change, some underlying values recur in culture after culture: the wish for freedom, independence and personal development, the striving to acquire property and to care for one's family and children, loyalty to a nation and its institutions. As Burke wrote to William Markham on November 9, 1771, "The principles that guide us in public and private, as they are not of our devising, but moulded into the nature and essence of things, will endure with the sun and moon."

The building of a tradition over many generations may be likened to the construction of a mighty reservoir. In his torrential *Speech on the Nabob of Arcot's Debts*, which exposed to Parliament the devastation visited upon India by the East India Company, Burke expatiated upon the subcontinent's system of reservoirs, constructed in "happier times" to make fertile and productive an otherwise parched region. He described how under native rule, religion, property and wealth in the northern province of the Carnatic were all directed to the husbanding of water. This tradition was quite unlike a European regimen, but it served its purpose of harbouring resources and maximizing productivity and security. "All ranks of people had their place in the public concern, and their share in the common stock and common prosperity." The reservoirs, he calculated, must in Tanjore and the Carnatic alone have numbered more than 10,000, excluding those for domestic use and religious purification.

> These are the monuments of real kings, who were the fathers of their people; testators to a posterity which they embraced as their own. These are the grand sepulchres built by ambition; but by the ambition of an insatiable benevolence, which, not contented with reigning in the dispensation of happiness during the contracted term of human life, had strained, with all the reachings and graspings of a vivacious mind, to extend the dominion of their bounty beyond the limits of nature, and to perpetuate themselves through generations of generations, the guardians, the protectors, the nourishers of mankind.

This is an extraordinary appreciation of an alien culture, from a man relying on books and reports and histories for his information. With the reachings and graspings of his own vivacious mind – his amazing imaginative sympathy – Burke extends his benevolence not only to a living generation of foreign people oppressed by his own, but to a remarkable praise of the long-dead benefactors of those natives. These fathers of the people he describes as themselves being mighty reservoirs: the nourishers of mankind for generation after generation. They were not content with serving immediate needs. They did not reign in their lifetimes only, because they did not rein in their benevolence to so short a span, but left monuments for the good of a long posterity. And still the fertility of Burke's peculiar pun is not exhausted (in a passage about inexhaustibility), for what the great kings were unsatisfied by was not the natural course of life, but the natural shortfall of *rain*. Their schemes came about because they were not contented with the rainfall, and wanted to extend the bounty of water beyond its short season. This they did, and wealth had accordingly cascaded down the generations. The good of their reigns was prolonged, like the good of the rains. Burke repeatedly uses words that evoke caricatures of despotic Indian princes – "ambition . . . insatiable . . . reachings and graspings . . . extend their dominion" – only to surprise his hearers when he says that the princes' ambitions were for the public benefit, and that the despoiling cupidity was the shameful characteristic rather of the transient British.

For now the reservoirs had been allowed to fall into miserable decay by those who did not appreciate, or care for, their importance. The British occupiers of India, like the French revolutionaries, thought they knew better and "introduced a new system". What ought to have been a permanent, self-renewing resource, needing only maintenance, was allowed to fail, and now the Indians were paying a terrible price. Once tradition has been neglected or breached, it is extremely difficult and costly to reconstruct. What is built with enormous effort may be lost with negligent ease.

Morally, the conventions we have inherited and learnt are where we start from. They save us from the impossible demand that in every situation we should rely on our own reason, moral sense and invention. Sometimes we know things intuitively, and trust our feelings without rational evidence. Personally, as we grow older, we learn from experience when to trust these intuitions, and certainly we may do so in emergencies, when we need to make quick judgments. Our prejudices are continuous with our skills; they are a form of "knowing exactly and habitually, without the labour of particular and occasional thinking" – to adopt Burke's words about the painter's art in a letter to the artist James Barry. Prejudices short-circuit thinking, sometimes for better, sometimes for worse.

Communally, the habits and disciplines of our many parents

allow us to delegate some responsibility to the past; they put us in touch with intuitions and responses which we might be unable to formulate for ourselves; they enable us to benefit from and to build upon others' experience. "Even in matters which are, as it were, just within our reach, what would become of the world," asks Burke, "if the practice of all moral duties, and the foundation of society, rested upon having their reasons made clear and demonstrative to every individual?"

Burke must have felt the force of this argument very directly, for it applies to much of his own work on the French Revolution. He had engaged himself precisely in the business of making demonstrative the reasons behind moral duties and the foundation of society. He articulates much that had been laid down or laid away in the collective subconscious, and that had now to be laid bare to oppose a reductive fundamentalism. He regretted that "all the decent drapery of life is to be torn off", but was forced to make propositionally explicit much that had been manifest only in practice, and which, he thought, properly belonged in the realm of the implicitly understood. "A few years ago," he writes, early in the *Reflections*, "I should be ashamed to overload a matter, so capable of supporting itself, by the then unnecessary support of any argument". When he sat down to write the letter which grew into that 364-page book, he can have had no idea how extensive it would become, how his ideas would ramify – "the matter gaining upon him" – and how he would find himself drawing out more and more from the recesses of his mind and heart. The strain must have been enormous. The result is the most personal and impassioned book about politics ever written.

In an age of reason, he became the spokesman for feeling. As a psychotherapist teases out the inner workings of an individual, Burke was trying to explain a whole society to itself. In these raids on the inarticulate, he was in a position not unlike that of Freud as he began to plumb the subconscious. "While I was thus at a loss," Freud said in the third of his Clark Lectures in the United States, "I clung to a prejudice the scientific justification for which was proved later by my friend C. G. Jung and his pupils in Zürich. I am bound to say it is sometimes most useful to have prejudices." Burke too knew that a full rational explication could not always be produced at once – or would not always satisfy – and that prejudices could in the meantime be useful in holding the line. "Every country wishing to preserve its liberty," he said in 1790, "must preserve its maxims."

The reserve of experience into which we feed and from which we draw is convention, or tradition – "the general bank and capital of nations, and of ages", Burke called it. If we have a proper sense of responsibility, we make this store of wisdom available to our children, and to theirs.

Tradition is not dead but alive in us. We do well to listen to our ancestral voices, taboos, scruples, hunches, intimations, inner promptings. The progressive tendency is to dismiss the claims of, say, conscience as mere prejudices. But prejudices can be anything but mere; they may be safeguarding our well-being. "An obstinate prejudice", wrote Keats in a letter begun on July 18, 1818, "can seldom be produced but from a gordian complication of feelings, which must take time to unravel and care to keep unravelled." Our knots of feelings cannot always be unpicked, but should rarely be cut through. Feelings may be less articulate than conscious thoughts, but this only means that we should attend to them more closely.

In his essay on "Burke and the Conservative Tradition", C. W. Parkin explains Burke's objection to 18th-century rationalism:

> If men realistically acknowledge the feebleness of human reason, and proceed with a due respect for what their predecessors have created and lived by, they can, he believes, be effective partners in their social destiny. But to assume that the truth has just come to light with oneself, after centuries of darkness, seems to Burke suicidal egotism. . . The inarticulate life of society, its customary, unthinking pattern of behaviour, not only must be admitted to be a great part of social existence; Burke insists that it is, in its own way, rational too. A man's instincts and feelings may sometimes guide him to his right end when his reason misleads or fails him. Likewise, widely shared, slowly evolved, tested traditions of behaviour represented a type of wisdom, which is available to everyone. . .

We ought, that is, to have a prejudice in favour of the traditional, on the ground that although its bases and reasonings may no longer or not yet be evident to us, it would have been unlikely to last – to have passed into tradition – if it were not effective and acceptable. Tradition is a form of winnowing, the survival through the ages of the best that has yet been devised. It is a human form of natural selection, a repository of provisional solutions.

Traditional criteria need not be static or complacent. They constitute a classical standard by which to measure the present and its innovations, but as Eliot wrote, "it is a judgment, a comparison, in which two things are measured by each other". Novelty should not easily displace the known, but should be put to the test of tradition; and yet tradition too should be continually scrutinized, for, in Eliot's words, "a tradition without intelligence is not worth having".

Writing about Burke's sense of "prescription", Paul Lucas describes how an immemorial constitution could be reconciled with an "accumulative idea of progress":

> Although the word "immemorial" often implied the words "static" and "unchanging" in content, this was not necessarily so. For lawyers like Matthew Hale, the ancient constitution was a complex and imperceptibly changing structure of customs that was being constantly tested by empirical experience, adapted to new situations, and refined in the law courts by decisions upon particular cases. Thus, the ancient constitution was both immemorial and up to date: it was a record of society's experience, and this record supported an empirical attitude in politics and political theory.
>
> ("On Edmund Burke's Doctrine of Prescription".)

Tradition need not be inflexible, but it provides a social norm, a behavioural default. How traditional tenets are applied is a matter for appraisal from time to time to time; but society does need such norms, for, again, there are not the resources to reason out every decision separately with philosophical rigour. Norms ensure some coherence and agreement, and are something against which nonconformism can be measured. For kinds of behaviour radiate outwards from the commonplace and conventional, through, say, the adventuruous, the bohemian, and the louche to the objectionable, the insane and the criminal. And to protect and sustain itself, a society needs to be able to measure degrees of the anti-social. Our system of legal and civil rights asserts that everyone who is not an undischarged criminal should always be treated equally; but this narrows the scope for discretion. People can be undesirable without breaking the law. Thomas Hamilton, who shot dead half of a class of young children in Dunblane in Scotland in 1996, had been regarded by many as suspicious, deviant, even potentially dangerous, yet he was allowed a gun licence, because nothing could be legally proven against him. Had the chief constable declined to sign his gun licence, Hamilton would have had a "right" to appeal against the decision. Yet society cannot rely for everything upon judicial and documentary standards of proof: personal judgment and discrimination are often appropriate. The issue is really whether a person is liable to violate not just the laws but the norms and traditions that hold us together.

A society without norms, which declares that every unorthodoxy is an equally valid "lifestyle choice" for the individual, gives itself no measures of or controls upon the abnormal. Without norms, deviation cannot be gauged. And if nothing is considered deviant, there is no way to distinguish, say, creative eccentricity from madness or dangerous perversion. Social norms assert that not everything is a matter of private choice, because some matters, some values, have already been decided and prescribed by society. Now, however, people are repeatedly told that life is a smorgasbord, all a matter of choice for the individual conscience. Our universities are iconoclastic, like the French National Assembly, and recommend to their youth "a study of the bold experimenters in morality", today under such labels as "deconstructionists". The only social value we are told we must hold to is not imposing our values on anyone else, but allowing them their "democratic" freedom to choose too. Yet for all this compulsory individualism, how few question the belief that every value and taboo should be questioned all the time.

Too much choice makes people unhappy. They are uncertain whether they will choose correctly, and so try to keep their options open indefinitely. Then they regret never having made up their minds – never having decided, for instance, what they want to do with their lives. Politicians say they wish to extend choice to all, yet there are already bewilderingly many choices for most of us. In the face of these, it would be appropriate first to prescribe discipline for all.

When Penguin Books was sensibly judged not to have broken the law by publishing *Lady Chatterley's Lover* in unexpurgated form, no one intended that hardcore pornography should become freely available. But instead of redrawing the line of acceptability, the courts and the public lost confidence in their ability to draw a line at all. What was shocking only to the prudish should never have been *illegal* (though it might not have been thought appropriate for the O-level syllabus), but abandoning virtually all restraints on the publication of indecent material has coarsened our feelings. Society has progressively abdicated its duty to discriminate, because it has lost faith in the idea of discrimination. Of course judgments of taste are not subject to rational proof, but as Burke tells us, society needs to agree values even though it may not be able to rationalize them. Taste and elegance he reckoned not as expendable subjective refinements, but "among the smaller and secondary morals". Granting a general indemnity is moral laziness.

Equally, when Parliament humanely legalized homosexual acts in the 1960s, it did not intend homosexuality to be seen as normal or natural. It was acting on compassionate considerations, just as Burke did in 1780, when, on his own initiative, he urged that the law which prescribed the pillory for convicted homosexuals be changed, after two offenders had been pelted to death. In the 1960s, when men were prey to blackmail for their sexual behaviour, palliation was evidently necessary; but by removing the sanction altogether, Parliament inadvertently removed the stigma. The effect was to reduce the degree to which homosexuality was thought deviant – and almost certainly to push some people who are sexually excited by the illicit to new extremes. A joke at the time ran: "It used to be the death penalty. Now it's legal. I'm leaving the country before it's made compulsory." And so, in a sense, it proved, as the newly legal practice became acceptable, was flaunted, and imperceptibly grew into a "right". Acceptance – if not the activity itself – "became compulsory" remarkably swiftly, as discrimination against homosexuals was outlawed. A norm of tolerant distaste and turning of blind eyes to what had been not only a sin but a crime, has in thirty years or so given way to a militant claim to parity and to a place in the armed services and the Church. People have been illiberally forced by progressives to accept explicit demonstrations of what was generally regarded as offensive, indecent or immoral. However open-minded we may be, not all sexual acts and not all "experiments in living" are equal; some, such as sado-masochism or rapacious promiscuity, are degrading, and it is against society's interests to permit them to seem normal. People, especially the young, the gullible and the vulnerable, need norms and standards so that they can judge prudently how to behave. That is why we need the courage of our conventions.

17

Nature

Whatever is traditional is likely to feel natural. Is it possible that this is sometimes because it goes with the grain not only of our society, but of our human being? Are our prejudices all random, learnt conventions, as the relativists tell us, or are some of them manifestations of our biology? We may find a tradition natural because the world and we have adapted to it: it may be a successful invention. But Burke believed that other traditions are innately suitable to the permanent conditions of the world and our position in it: that they are discoveries.

"Nature" is a term highly contentious and rightly suspect (though much appealed to, especially since the age of revolutionaries and Romantics). Arguments such as whether man is "naturally" good or evil and about "nature" versus "nurture" grow ever more elaborate but come no nearer to resolution.

People have long known that the term "nature" is an imprecise metaphor that is hard to avoid. Dr Johnson's primary definition is "An imaginary being supposed to preside over the material and animal world." The word's significations are "so various, and so difficultly defined" that after twelve definitions he adds an epitome of Robert Boyle's *Free Enquiry into the Receiv'd Notion of Nature* (1685), ending with a warning: "*Nature* is sometimes indeed commonly taken for a kind of semi-deity. In this sense it is best not to use it at all." Certainly as grounds for assertion and appeal, like "self-evident" or Paine's "Common Sense", it is intellectually empty. What is naturally and self-evidently common sense to one man is the opposite to another. Yet for the proponents of revolution, empty, unspecific terms were useful: people could fill the vacuum with whatever meaning suited their personal wishes and so everyone would seem, for a time, to be supporting the same cause. But despite the aspirations of the *philosophes*, what is natural is not apparent from *a priori* reasoning; the term acquires force only when it is backed by the evidence of endurance, by evidence that generations have agreed upon something. They may all be wrong, but unnatural traditions (such as incest) tend to destroy themselves.

In his book *The End of Nature*, Bill McKibben makes the case that nothing is natural any more – certainly not our landscapes, seas, weather, atmosphere, plants, animals, genes or societies – so that any appeal to nature is naïve and without a referent. There is no "force of nature"; only the force of circumstances. It is a fallacy to believe that a benign nature will ameliorate or regulate conditions on Earth. Nature is not an external, unchanging or self-correcting reality, but a bundle of dispositions, emotions and projections, stemming from the efforts of species to survive.

There is much in this case, although one need not agree when McKibben goes on to argue that having intervened in the planet's ecosystems we must now take charge of everything we used to think of as natural, and must try to manage the fate of the Earth. For this is akin to the idea that once the state has interfered in any aspect of society or the economy, it must manage it forever. On the contrary, a benevolent neglect may turn out to be the best policy with, say, an oil spill, just as with telecommunications or exchange rates.

Furthermore, arrogant attempts to manipulate systems that we do not fully understand – which means almost all systems – have a tendency to push them beyond their tolerance. By leaving conventional methods far behind, the agri-business, for instance, has increased farm productivity enormously, at least for the present; but as the worldwide dominance of a handful of staple crops has massively increased, alarm has spread about the loss of genetic diversity. And while the artificial comes naturally to man, it does not to cows and sheep. Against their inclination ruminant animals have been turned into carnivores and even cannibals, probably increasing the risk of epidemics. Man's old contract with the soil and with other species has been pushed aside. Within just a generation or so, the feeling for the natural – in the sense of what was long tried and successful – has virtually been abandoned.

Burke himself spent many hours on his farmland at Beaconsfield, and corresponded with the agriculturalist Arthur Young about the most scientific methods of cultivation. Among some manuscript anecdotes about him, now in Boston Public Library, is a note: "Edmund Burke told young Abraham Shackleton that he thought people did well to try experiments in farming, that they might find the old way to be the best." There is an Irish slyness about the phrasing: experimentation will discover not only what is best, but that what is best is already known and therefore no discovery.

The old ways are the best ways, they say. Well, they aren't, always; but like the saying, they have a recurrent, rule-of-thumb applicability. Even evident anachronisms may turn out to have lasted for good reasons. British Crown Court and High Court judges, for instance, still wear wigs in the style that almost everyone else gave up at the end of the 18th century. Some people condemn the practice as absurd and irrational, and wish them to abandon it. But while wigs may have been adopted centuries ago as a fashion, they turn out to have unintended benefits in court. Costume marks out the law courts (like churches) as special places of dignity and ritual. Questionings there are not casual and everyday matters, but are invested with particular powers. The whole and solemn truth is required by the majesty of the law. Additionally, wigs impersonalize the proceedings. A bewigged judge is sitting not as an individual, but as an impartial officer of the state (like the bewigged Speaker in the Commons). He must be as objective as possible. Which judge tries which case should not matter: they should be as alike as possible. As justice should be uniform, so justices should be uniformed. Biographical details and personal tastes or beliefs must be suppressed. The judge's personal appearance is immaterial. With the wig, he takes on a particular role, which makes him different from the man who catches the train home after the case. And furthermore, wigs make judges less individually recognizable, reducing the chances of vendettas against them. As Burke writes in the *Reflections*, there is a great difference "between what policy would dictate on the original introduction of such institutions, and on a question of their total abolition where they have cast their roots wide and deep, and where by long habit things more valuable than themselves are so adapted to them, and in a manner inwoven with them, that one cannot be destroyed without impairing the other."

Incidental advantages and an inherited sense of fitness mean we should be wary about disrupting patterns of behaviour that have worked well over long periods. It may be useful to think of the natural this way, as what is habitual or well-tried. Michael Oakeshott argued that our civilized inheritance "is a world not because it has any meaning (it has none), but because it is a whole of interlocking meanings which establish and interpret one another." The meaning lies in the use; and, as Wordsworth wrote, "The mild necessity of use compels To acts of love". This neatly answers the reductive, deconstructionist assertion that if values are man-made they are random and that any others would do as well. For this to be true, we should have to discard *all* of our cultural values, Oakeshott's "world". Yet Oakeshott perhaps conceded too much. Even artifices that are acknowledged as artificial may work uniquely well and satisfy something within us that is as yet too deep for explication. It may be that long ago, someone, somehow, discovered the genius of the thing.

The artificial is not necessarily arbitrary, and need not always be contrasted with the natural, for as Burke neatly put it, "Art is man's nature". But art had better keep nature in mind. Undoubtedly we *feel* that certain things are fitting and profoundly in harmony. Bach's music sounds harmonious; twelve-tone music does not. This is not a matter of opinion but a psychological fact, and although it may be mysterious, it is important. Pythagoras discovered the mathematical ratios on which classical musical intervals depend, but could not explain their "rightness". There is likely, however, to be a reason for this which we have still not fully understood. Many old wives' tales and superstitions once dismissed as irrational have later been shown to be based upon homespun science. The tuning of pianos may seem to be an artificial convention, but the appeal of harmony is not man-made or negligible, and deserves more respect than Stockhausen, for instance, has paid it.

Burke was always interested in these ideas. He had dealt with them in his *Philosophical Enquiry into the Origin of our Ideas of the Sublime and Beautiful*, which he may have begun planning while still at college. The 20th-century art historian E. H. Gombrich says this book was the first to try "to base our aesthetic response on psychology, or even on our biology". He explains how it can be so: "Consider the liking for glitter: a child likes it, a pearly-king likes it; it is probably universal. In that respect, the diatonic system of music is a discovery of what appeals" (*Oxford Magazine* No 123,

Michaelmas 1995). Our biology predisposes us to gravitate towards certain things; there are stirrings within us as surely as within migrating birds.

The colour green is especially restful to human beings, for which we should be thankful because it is very common. This psychological nuance may be providence or just luck (it may always have been so); or man may have gradually adapted to the colour's ubiquity. Whichever it is, there is now a happy coinciding of our predilection and the external world. Such things can meaningfully be termed natural to us. So Burke's appeals to human nature, or natural justice, need not be dismissed as 18th-century sentimentality. He is not appealing to abstractions, but to observable constants in human behaviour and history, to "human nature; either as that nature is universal, or as it is modified by local habits and social aptitudes" (our second nature). In speaking of nature, "which is wisdom without reflection, and above it", he refers to preferences and patterns that have arisen spontaneously, not to what he feels ought to exist.

Some traditional practices can be rationalized only in terms of their effectiveness. The history of medicine provides examples of drugs and treatments which were used before they were understood, because they were found to work (though also of others which were long employed before finally being abandoned as useless, such as blood-letting). We need not argue whether such treatments are natural or artificial. Their practical consequences should decide their value. Medical problems do not primarily concern truth or falsehood. They relate to illness or health. What in the result is likely to make people ill is medically false: that which is productive of health, medically is true. A doctor may justifiably use a technique that brings relief even though he does not know how it works. To condemn this as prejudice, rather than investigating the phenomenon would be retrograde. And Burke offers the same empirical, anti-theoretical measure of political and social health:

> The practical consequences of any political tenet go a great way in deciding upon its value. Political problems do not primarily concern truth or falsehood. They relate to good or evil. What in the result is likely to produce evil is politically false: that which is productive of good, politically is true.
>
> (*Appeal to the Old Whigs.*)

Like medicines, certain social and political institutions may be more than random inventions to which we have become accustomed. They may be native to us, deep discoveries – like the fitness of marriage, which is universally practised in human societies. Burke believed that the existing order in Europe sprang from permanent elements in human nature, and that Britain's political system was "in a just correspondence and symmetry with the order of the world". Such structures, like musical harmony, may feel natural because they correspond to some property of our being. By contrast, unnatural systems, such as communism, which take too little account of human strengths and weaknesses, passions and aspirations, seem eventually to collapse under their own weight. However forcefully or benignly they may be imposed, they do not become natural. The graft is rejected.

But even if harmony exists only within systems, and does not represent a correspondence between them and the external world, it can still be maintained or breached. Different languages, for instance, contain distinct and harmonious systems in their grammars, their puns and rhymes, in particular felicities, words related etymologically or by classic usage – and it is possible to work with or against this "genius of the language". New words or constructions may be felt to jar, because they disturb the pattern. "Subsidiarity", to take a far-from-random example, is a word that feels shifty, because its usage is forced: it is used to denote not "the quality of being subsidiary" (*OED*), but an insincere political doctrine imposed, paradoxically, from the centre of the European Union. And despite the word's pseudo-scientific sound, its gawkiness gives it away. It doesn't fit the English language. It feels, and is, dishonest – about as far from Burke's small cells of authority as it is possible to get. Our sense of the pattern of the language and of what is indigenous to it warns us to beware of this misbegotten mistranslation. It is not possible to tell the truth in such terms.

Similarly, some attempts to introduce new elements into our social arrangements will be felt as distortions which unbalance the whole. Within a particular system, some innovations will be psychologically disturbing. The idea, for instance, of "homosexual marriage" cannot be reconciled with our feeling about what marriage is. "Homosexual marriage" is a travesty. It is unnatural. To accept the practice, or the term, would be to alter the meaning of true marriage. What Eliot wrote in 1917 about the introduction into a culture of a new work of art applies also to this kind of innovation: "The existing order is complete before the new work arrives; for order to persist after the supervention of novelty, the *whole* existing order must be, if ever so slightly, altered." For a homosexual pair to "marry" is not a private matter between two people alone, but reorders society; it necessarily affects attitudes to marriage, reducing the significance of a bond that is widely held to be unique and intrinsically bound up with procreation. In the first of his *Letters on a Regicide Peace*, Burke reviles the French Constituent Assembly for attempting to desecrate and degrade marriage by pronouncing it "no better than a common, civil contract", and notes that this has led to a divorce rate in Paris of one marriage in three. To him and to many people now, a threat to the institution of marriage is a threat to all of society.

C. S. Lewis explains what is wrong with homosexuality by describing what is right with heterosexual love:

> But in the act of love we are not merely ourselves. We are also representatives. It is here no impoverishment but an enrichment to be aware that forces older and less personal than we work through us. In us all the masculinity and femininity of the world, all that is assailant and responsive, are momentarily focused . . . within the rite or drama they become a god and goddess between whom there is no equality – whose relations are asymmetrical.
>
> (*The Four Loves*.)

Marriage is about difference as much as sameness. It is a coupling of complementaries. Homosexuals cannot complete one another in the same way, because so much – an entire gender – is excluded from their partnerships, and because they cannot send their entwined genes spiralling into the future. Homosexuality may be ingrained in some people's make-up, as may other aberrations, but if society ceases to regard it as an aberration, the norm of the family is weakened. The claim that relations between members of the same sex are not necessarily different from those between the sexes attempts to homogenize men and women, and this affects everyone.

Consider, then, the defining relation between the sexes. A prejudice tells us that sexuality is naturally a private and privileged matter, and that it has to do with familial love. In exploring the reciprocity of male and female, we seem to glimpse the meaning of our being, and learn to give of ourselves. Sex should be pleasurable, of course, but is not just for pleasure, for it has an overwhelming significance. Perhaps man's fundamental achievement is the apprehension, so acute in sex, that he is more than beast. As John Donne writes in "The Extasie", we feel that our bodies "are ours, though they are not wee", for there is a spirit too: "That subtile knot, which makes us man".

All this feels indelible, innate, native, because this is the way we are made. As Ian McEwan puts it in his novel *The Child in Time*, "biology, existence, matter itself had dreamed this up for its own pleasure and perpetuity, and this was exactly what you were meant to do, it wanted you to like it." The match of behaviour and feeling is inwardly fulfilling.

Sexual love draws upon long experience, and plays it out once again. "Lying together there goes back so far," wrote Philip Larkin, "An emblem of two people being honest." Now it is our turn to continue the old, mutating and recombining design – the same genes man has always had, in a pattern different from any seen before – and to pass on life's mystery to others.

Burke writes beautifully of marriage as "the contract that renovates the world". His phrase is perfect because it fits so well with our feelings. Sex literally restocks and rejuvenates the world by peopling it; but it renovates and redeems men and women too: refreshing them and their feelings for one another. In both making us anew and making new people, sex gives the world a fresh and innocent start.

It also promotes mutual dependence – and for a purpose. We reveal to one another what it is of ourselves that we otherwise most protect, each delivering up what is most vulnerable in exchange for an implicit undertaking to protect that part of the other. Sex has a unique power to involve us in one other, to marry our fortunes together. As Paul Simon sings, with a proper coyness, "When they wake up, they will find All their personal belongings have intertwined". Or John Donne again:

> Love, these mixt soules, doth mix againe,
> And makes both one, each this and that.
>
> ("The Extasie".)

What might otherwise be a selfish desire is redeemed by the solicitude that is family feeling. Naked and needy, babytalking and looking babies, we are at our most baby-like, and the act of love is emotionally, or spiritually, sympathetic to the transmission of life.

Rather as a real violation of a person's body or liberty dwarfs the claims of bogus "human rights" or "civil rights", so love belongs to a different class from its simulacra. To find someone with whom one desires to make children is to see into the future and to discover a deeper meaning in sex than is otherwise possible. This is why homosexuality is a thwarting, a failure to find the ultimate fulfilment. It is a deliberate attempt to break one of our deepest psychological templates (and one which is present in children). Such behaviour can rightly be described as deviant, because there is a norm from which it knowingly deviates. Donne remarks in *Biathanatos* that this "sin against nature" is abominable precisely because "the knowledge thereof is so domestic, so near, so inward to us". There is no mistaking what sex is for. All this is not to endorse the narrow idea that reproduction is the sole purpose of sex, and so that contraception is always wrong; sex, the completest intercourse, is also about engendering and expressing love. But this *is* the proper place for children to be made. What is most essential in us, the stuff we are made from, is passed on in this highly-charged context, where our bodies and imaginations do everything possible to bind us to one another and to teach us to cherish the child.

Love for a child entails wanting to make the world better for him or her, to provide what we missed, to protect and nurture. And this, to a degree that can never be overstated, is what children need. So the pattern can go on repeating. It is successful, natural to us, which is why we are here.

Yet science has made sex possible without procreation, and more recently made procreation possible without sex. We can uncouple the cart from the horse, cutting through the knot of feelings and salutary prejudices.

Sex without procreation – easily available contraception – once seemed to be sheer gain, but it has had insidious effects.

> When I see a couple of kids
> And guess he's fucking her and she's
> Taking pills or wearing a diaphragm,
> I know this is paradise
>
> Everyone old has dreamed of all their lives –

writes Philip Larkin in "High Windows", saddened for both old and young. Reliable contraception has made sex less of a risk, and the bitterness in his lines is partly due to genuine envy of those born later; but it is a tawdry paradise in which love is reduced to fucking, and even fucking is debased by the mechanics of pills and diaphragms. Can this really be what everyone old has dreamed of – "bonds and gestures pushed to one side"? Larkin knows that this is separating things that ought not to be separated, abstracting sex from its proper context.

And while contraception has made sex easier, it has perhaps made bonds and gestures harder, and made men and women less satisfied with their lives. There is, to begin with, the nagging worry that there is lots of sex on offer, and that one is missing out. Then there is the disappointment of sex without bonds and gestures. In casual sex, people learn to isolate themselves from the risks of emotional intimacy, with the result that they may later find they are unable to commit themselves. Sex is properly compromising in every sense; but the promiscuous learn how not to be compromised, and so forget how to make compromises. Instead, they become Burke's "calculators". As they repeatedly betray or are betrayed, they train themselves in cynicism. Remaining self-possessed means never giving oneself away, never giving away one's self; and yet part of us longs for that ecstatic freedom.

Instead, contraception has lowered the stakes by offering a lesser freedom. Some other girl looks attractive too, so why not give her a whirl? And as people become more promiscuous, sex becomes less special – less of a commitment. The rite of passage which used to make people grow up is less important, and more people never do. Yet sexual adepts expect much more, and have more partners to compare. So whilst enjoying the technique of one, they reflect wistfully and secretly on the physique of another and the caresses of a third. Less than contented, they are the more liable to stray in search of the impossible someone who will satisfy all of their longings. Additionally, the extension of choice tends to make people more neurotic about their own appearance and less happy with themselves. Chastity, which everyone old dreamed of escaping, turns out to have had its long-term advantages.

Just as widespread dependable contraception separated sex from procreation, so medical techniques have made babies available without sex. Children who are the products of technology may be as much wanted as any, and more than some. Nevertheless, babies created in a laboratory or born out of an imposter's womb are a defiance of biology and that pattern which makes sense of our existence. Individual cases may be welcomed, and yet there is an emotional and social risk in abstracting reproduction from sex, and it produces an instinctive revulsion. A mother's embrace ought to begin before birth. The physical connection literally ties the child to the mother, so that every generation in human history is bound, like a team of climbers, by a single rope. What must it be to be born without that attachment and security?

That cord, furthermore, symbolizes the primary dependence of a child's life, on its mother. The importunity of the blood cannot be ignored, and the child makes its earliest demands by influencing the mother's hormones. An infant needs to be loved and nurtured not by someone, but by the body it came from. In the early months and years, it needs security every minute: maternal intensive care. The love of a mother for her child is unique, so close that the father might be jealous if he were not dotingly proud of both of them – and, rather comically, of himself.

Most people, fortunately, are chilled by the rationalism of the writer of a letter to *The Guardian* who was quite prepared to countenance the exclusion of fathers altogether, and who tried to balance "the pros and cons of sexual intercourse versus artificial insemination as alternative ways to make babies" by pointing out that "the traditional method . . . has the downside of being potentially painful or embarrassing to do, is affected in quantity and possibly quality by tiredness, stress and diet, and is difficult for other people to help with". Nonetheless, increasing numbers of women are making their selfish calculations and deciding to leave men out of their lives. Babies are beginning to be seen as a woman's "right", a commodity to which any woman in any circumstances is entitled if she chooses, or which she is entitled not to have if she chooses. Babies are considered to be attributes of their mothers, as if unrelated to fathers, and as if they had no independent future. The discussion in 1996 about the ethics of a mother aborting one twin because bringing up two was more than she fancied was conducted with scarcely a thought for the possible lifelong feelings of the survivor. Immediately afterwards, huge publicity was afforded to the case of an unmarried mother, with one child already, who had been given fertility treatment resulting in a pregnancy of eight foetuses. This presented a grotesque dilemma, because doctors advised that it would be impossible for them all to be born alive. The mother was accordingly urged to submit to an arbitrary cull, but refused, and meanwhile a newspaper offered her money as a freak show. The situation was repulsive, inhuman, unnatural, and was the fault of a treatment which frequently results in multiple pregnancies and which should not have been prescribed. To offer a treatment that is likely to make necessary a selective slaughter of foetuses in this way is wicked.

A week later, the newspapers told the story of a woman who by the age of 21 had been pregnant five times and who was seeking publicly funded fertility treatment so that she and her boyfriend – both unemployed – could have children. Her five pregnancies had resulted in two abortions and three children, who had had to be adopted because of allegations that both her father and her former husband were involved in "child abuse". She wanted treatment because her fallopian tubes had been damaged by a sexually transmitted disease. Public discussion pitted her "right" to have children at will against the predictable expense to the state and the likely unhappy consequences. Yet the liberal terms of discussion are inadequate here. The underlying question is: what causes these appalling situations? What has society done or forgotten that produces them?

In the *Reflections*, Burke warned that "the people must not be suffered to imagine that their will is the standard of right and wrong". Our duties and obligations have little to do with our wishes. In the *Appeal to the Old Whigs* he writes: "Duties are not voluntary. Duty and will are even contradictory terms." In the pursuit of individual fulfilment and so-called "reproductive rights", many people have forgotten their duties, and lost all humility. The mistake is to imagine that one or other value or "right" can operate in a vacuum, overriding all other considerations, moral or practical. We value freedom, so no one's choices must ever be restricted. Children are a blessing, so all births, however wretched, must be good. Every life should have a chance of fulfilment, so no gratification must ever be denied. People should be treated fairly, so we may never discriminate between those deserving of help and those not. Prejudice can blind us to the facts, so we must expunge all of our inherited beliefs. But values and virtues are not scientific laws; beyond some point they turn upon themselves and produce evil. They lead to behaviour that is at odds with our deepest sense of propriety.

In this light, the sexual revolution looks like a violation of human nature. It did not establish new norms. On the contrary, as the erotic and reproductive possibilities have expanded and gone their separate ways, morality has been privatized, so that society's stake in our sexual behaviour is now too little acknowledged. We are caught somewhere between the old sexual rules and a supposed new freedom.

One very damaging effect of being in this limbo is semi-consenting promiscuity. Very few women boast of promiscuity. Most of those who are promiscuous are uneasy about it because they are aware of residual taboos and ideals. They also feel from their own experience that promiscuity is unsatisfactory. So while they may allow men to have their way, perhaps after drinking too much, they do not fully consent or take responsibility. This makes the sex unsatisfactory, hypocritical, half-hearted at best, and leaves the man to bear all the responsibility – unsure whether he has done the right thing. If the woman is unable to give of herself, neither she nor her partner knows whether he has done more than take selfish advantage. What should be a meeting and a mingling is instead a standoff. At worst, sex feels, on both sides, like an assault.

> The time is now propitious, as he guesses,
> The meal is ended, she is bored and tired,
> Endeavours to engage her in caresses
> Which still are unreproved, if undesired.
> Flushed and decided, he assaults at once;
> Exploring hands encounter no defence;
> His vanity requires no response,
> And makes a welcome of indifference.

Eliot's description of peremptory "Exploring hands" is a travesty of the feeling of life-changing, world-expanding discovery described by Donne in "To his Mistris Going to Bed":

> Licence my roaving hands, and let them go,
> Before, behind, between, above, below.
> O my America! my new-found-land,
> My kingdome, safeliest when with one man man'd. . .

Donne's imagination soars; he makes the grandest claims, and he breaks new ground (not least by writing a line that consists entirely of prepositions). But Eliot's unimaginative young man is not exploring a new world. He is neither excited nor overwhelmed, merely "flushed". He does not much care whether the woman is with one man man'd, or with many. Instead of working up to a moment of joy, he waits until she is "bored and tired" – a time which he calculates is "propitious". The moment may be favourable to his "assault", but it is very unfavourable to true intercourse. The encounter is never positive, but is framed by negatives: "unreproved . . . undesired . . . no defence . . . no response . . . indifference". The woman neither consents by taking part nor resists. Her attitude is "half-formed": "'Well now that's done: and I'm glad it's over.'"

Instead of offering release, such encounters build up tensions and guilts between the sexes. Men begin to feel that rather than sharing and being involved with women, they are getting the better of them. The urge which will not go away becomes exploitative, as men seek not to make love, but to "score" over women. One of the most powerful of human forces is used not to unite us, but to force us apart. Not finding affection and acceptance of their needs, men become more assertive and accept a more brutal role. If it has to be assault, to use Eliot's unlovely term, so be it. If women make men feel that sex is an attack, then there will be more sexual attacks. This is not excusable but it is explicable.

So-called "liberation" can be more damaging than repression. For instance, to describe today's immodest, erotic fashions and pervasive lascivious imagery as "the sexual empowerment of women" is dangerously mistaken. Women have always exerted enormous sexual power over men. Male libido is among the strongest of urges, and needs not to be provoked and further aroused in public, but to be kept in check. Consequently, societies have traditionally developed codes of shame to mark off private behaviour from public, and to tame and channel the sexual drive. Increasingly, however, these are disregarded; no one, for instance, is any longer condemned for "looking like a tart". But as women let it all hang out, and public acceptability changes, control over men's libido is being lost. Without codes of decency and honour – which Burke lamented, but which have since been ridiculed as irrational or patronizing – women can become the victims of an overwhelming force. And yet the victims may well not be the glamorous who are comfortable exposing themselves, but the less assertive and more vulnerable. It is not in women's interests if sex has lost its mystery, its privacy and its intimacy with romance, or if chivalry is allowed to die.

The prolonged union of marriage has been a successful artifice because it satisfies, sophisticates and restrains our sexual urges. It is an achievement not just of the couple immediately concerned, but of society. Marriage, Burke wrote, "is the origin of all relations, and consequently the first element of all duties". Christianity, by imposing an indissoluble monogamy, had, he continued, "done more towards the peace, happiness, settlement, and civilization of the world, than . . . any other part in this whole scheme of divine wisdom." But once marriage begins to break down, fewer people have before them in their own families successful models to follow – and for them, rising above the impulses of lust is the more difficult. Although falling in love is as popular as ever, many people have forgotten, or never learnt, how to love and to sustain love. Something valuable is in danger of being lost.

"It is not necessary", wrote Burke, "to observe upon the horrible consequences of taking one half of the species wholly out of the guardianship and protection of the other." Women now routinely react to this as though it were offensive. They assume that it means only that women need protecting by men, and are quick to reject the idea. A few years ago Burke might have been accused of condescending "male chauvinism", but this term, criticizing an attitude, has now almost disappeared, to be replaced by a harder thing, an offence against ideology, the thought-crime of "sexism". All this, however, is a narrowing and a misunderstanding. Burke was just as aware of the reciprocal need that men have to be protected by women. The sexes, he is saying, need one another, and a proper society between them serves the interests of both. Yet today, instead of this mutuality, there is often contempt, a "sex war" in which women's magazines militantly ask "What are men for?" Many women refuse to allow themselves to be protected by men, and have withdrawn the particular protection – that sense of belonging and of having a home – which men need. The crucial security of one another's arms ("to have and to hold") is no longer to be relied upon and some couples even agree pre-emptive divorce terms before they marry. Both sexes are more vulnerable. That place of retreat, our special, private place in the world, is insecure. But without it and the shared candour that we there enjoy, we are straitened – no more than our separate selves. For all of the rushing around trying to fit everything into a busy life, a dimension is felt to be missing. With more and more women at work full-time, there is ever less of a world elsewhere into which to withdraw for respite from money-making and ambition. Our private lives are losing their domesticity and becoming ever more like business transactions. The cross-graining of society is being lost. "What chiefly remains of the new freedom is its meagre impoverished emotional life," wrote T. S. Eliot, ahead of his time.

Today, many partnerships are arrangements of convenience, within which men and women primarily remain individuals, looking for gain without sacrifice. Symbolically, women decline to give up their maiden names for the sake of establishing a new unity (it makes separation so much less messy). Responsibilities to one another and to future generations are shirked. And this is far from a private problem: it is one of the most disruptive of the West's present discontents. Because we idolize personal freedoms, we are reluctant as a society to enforce, or even uphold, particular values; yet society has an overwhelming interest in its own future, and cannot afford to refuse all moral judgments. "The passion called love," wrote Burke in his *Letter to a Member of the National Assembly*, "has so general and powerful an influence; it makes so much of the entertainment, and indeed so much the occupation of that part of life which decides the character for ever, that the mode and the principles on which it engages the sympathy, and strikes the imagination, become of the utmost importance to the morals and manners of every society."

It used to be that a woman would willingly sacrifice some opportunities in (say) her career, in return for a man's willingly remaining faithful and supporting her and their children. Women, it was said, would have sex in order to get married, while men would get married in order to have sex. Now, as this age-old bargain collapses, ever more men are having sex without facing their consequent responsibilities, and women are having children (within marriage or without) and not facing theirs either. Some men have always exploited women for sexual gratification. This does not excuse some women's now exploiting men by using them and discarding them, simply to produce children. Sex has its responsibilities; reproduction has even more, and if people are to be adults, they must accept them. Instead, society is becoming infantilized.

The creative and enabling job of sustaining and upholding families is the foundation of fulfilling and worthwhile lives. In the past, much of it was women's work, a continual effort that was "never done", and which in many cases was insufficiently supported by men. Few women were paid for it directly, though this does not mean its importance was not appreciated. But in recent decades women have begun to decry and undervalue it, and thereby themselves. Through pride or distrust, they have begun to think of themselves as sovereign individuals who ought to have (or had better have) careers, and whose work must be paid for in cash. So now much of this invaluable work of cohesion is, in another sense, never done. Children, after all, cannot pay for their mothers' efforts: their well-being, to state the forgotten obvious, requires values such as duty and love, currencies other than money.

An immemorial agreement has been fractured but not renegotiated. This is a disaster for both sexes, for trust between them, for families, and for society. It is simplistic to condemn the old relations as though they had always and exclusively belittled women. An improved accommodation requires acknowledgment of those elements of our permanent relations which answer a need on both sides. But the very idea of mutual interests is now often denied. Men are said to have connived in the bad old ways by *pretending* they were human nature, even though it cannot plausibly be argued that monogamy is a male imposition upon women. Saying that the roles which generations of mothers and fathers accepted were parts of a repressive convention trumped up for a sectional advantage is like arguing that the diatonic scale is a conspiracy of composers. The harmony is more likely to be of the nature of things. Innocent of sexual politics, children still just want their mothers. A social pattern which is as innate in us as the twists of DNA is being sacrificed to an insistence on equality which contrives to forget that people can be equal but different, different but complementary. This is yet one more example of destruction of the existing order in favour of "a theoretic experimental edifice" which turns out to have grave disadvantages. Mankind has evolved in certain ways under certain pressures over thousands of generations. We cannot develop radically new patterns in a generation or two without severe penalties. Indeed Burke believes that we are not free to construct and vary our domestic relations as we may think fit:

> When we marry, the choice is voluntary, but the duties are not matter of choice. They are dictated by the nature of the situation. Dark and inscrutable are the ways by which we come into the world. The instincts which give rise to this mysterious process of nature are not of our making. But out of physical causes, unknown to us, perhaps unknowable, arise moral duties, which, as we are able perfectly to comprehend, we are bound indispensably to perform.
>
> (*Appeal to the Old Whigs.*)

A child's mother inescapably begins the work of rearing. From her the infant learns the mother tongue and lessons at mother's knee. Father tongue and father's knee are not the same. Nor, for all its swelling pride, is father's breast. Men do not produce milk, and they make poor mothers. The bringing up of children, the most important and intensive work in the world, is largely women's work. Children learn at an extraordinary rate in their first years – a rate never to be matched – and they do this best within the context of a nurturing female security continuous with the total protection from which they have just emerged. A father's love is differently crucial. It is less physically intimate, and part of the father's role is to induce the child's sense of independence. The child has to be able to distinguish himself as an individual, to separate from mother, and to relate to others. The father is the first completely new human being.

Certainly women should not settle for second-best in life – and every decent man wants women's lives to be as rewarding as his own. Women should be well educated, have wide interests and many friends, and should contribute to almost every aspect of life (excepting the most brutal and physical tasks). It is all the better, for mother and children, if women can work at home (which includes the most artistic and creative occupations), or telecommute, or work for themselves, or others, or help to run a family concern.

Society relies upon women to do things that men cannot do so well. First among these is childbearing and nurturing the young, but women are generally better at most other forms of emotional support. They are intensely observant about other people and are good at working without ulterior motives – for, as it used to be said, love. Less selfish than men, they are more able to see when glory or status is irrelevant and something is its own reward. They are better at seeing things in the round and as they relate. They have always been involved in – and have mostly run – the many activities, associations and institutions that bind neighbourhoods and the wider society, and which must co-exist with the other kind of business. Women are, for instance, vital to charities, to magistrates' courts, in organizing advisory services and in the thousand informal relations and intricacies that Burke saw are crucial to the civil constitution. And these networks are important not least to women when they become mothers, so that they can lean upon one another, and have time to escape the infant tyranny. But all this does not mean that women must do everything that men do. Men, after all, cannot do everything women can (and may reasonably feel some imaginative sadness about that).

If duty – putting one's obligations before one's present wishes – has any meaning, then a mother's duty to her child is fundamental. In his *Dictionary*, Dr Johnson defines duty first as "that to which a man is by any natural or legal obligation bound", and goes on to quote Locke: "The pain children feel from any necessity of nature, it is the duty of parents to relieve." Like charity, duty begins at home. Parents – men as well as women – should put their own wishes second to the absolute needs of their children (as, ideally, did their parents), and this will always entail a particular engagement on the part of the mother. Proper mothering is simply incompatible with spending eight hours a day away from young children. But then bringing up children is a job of infinitely greater significance than most careers.

Lots of women are not "free" to work; they have no choice but to. They are trapped in jobs as surely as their mothers or grandmothers were trapped at home. Some women are principal or sole earners, and with families being postponed, careers come first for many in both chronology and priority. With so many mothers working, this is now largely accepted. Not wishing to make rude personal criticisms, we decline to stigmatize this new pattern. On the contrary, we have made the old pattern less and less viable by equality legislation. This has driven up women's pay, theoretically to match that of men. Unable to afford this, employers have held down men's pay, so that it is less likely to be adequate to support a wife and family. This means that women are forced to work outside the home, and the roles of men and women are made less distinct. Equality laws have not simply extended opportunities for those women who want them; they have forced a generation of women to live in a particular way, whether they wish to or not.

Worse even than being trapped in a job is being trapped on "benefit". Many single mothers, in the absence of their children's fathers, have to try to fulfil both roles, and are incapable of doing so. Instead of enjoying the support of a man, they have to fight a capricious, soul-destroying bureaucracy for their weekly handout, which enables them to exist but not to live. Their only company may be the children, with their enormous demands. The result is often short-temper and squalor. Rather than bringing the children up properly, as they intended, mothers find themselves swearing and lashing out. The children are at first cowed, then brutalized, then themselves aggressive and uncontrollable in adolescence.

Women's obsession with how to meet all the demands upon them (and unease about failing to do so) is evidence that trying to do everything for themselves is an unnatural strain. The pieces do not fit. Many women seem to react to this by becoming the more ruthless, but there are also anecdotal signs of increasing dissatisfaction with a feminism that rejects femininity. Responding to a survey which found that women have begun to acquire aggressive or arrogant male characteristics, while men are becoming feminized, Fay Weldon was quoted as saying: "I think a lot of women, at least middle-class women, are beginning to accept that although our role in the past may have been boring, women were nevertheless better off when they weren't in the labour market but were staying at home and looking after the children. Women have had enough of this liberation lark, having to go to work to pay the bills. Mature women are finally coming to realise that the attraction between men and women lies in our differences" (*Daily Mail*, July 22, 1996).

Official policy, however, is still to ignore these differences. Most strikingly, the Ministry of Defence has proposed that women should be allowed to serve in war in combat roles. This would be the ultimate breach with what Burke called the "salutary domestic prejudice", and a letter to *The Sunday Telegraph* (July 14, 1996) eloquently expressed why it would have barbaric repercussions. Foremost among our civilized values, wrote the correspondent, is respect for and the protection of women, and the willingness of men to fight for the security of their wives and families. The ministry's proposals, however,

> would legitimize women killing, and being killed, in war. Inevitably, the brutalization of attitudes would be transposed to society as a whole. Can society face with equanimity the impact of thousands of women – including wives and mothers – being killed in some future Somme or Normandy or Vietnam? . . . The shock to value systems would be gravely damaging.

"I thought ten thousand swords must have leaped from their scabbards to avenge even a look that threatened her with insult," wrote Burke. "Oh! what a revolution!"

What goes on in the family in the early years of life is a great trust. The earliest learning is not conscious, but subliminal. What an infant learns becomes second nature. These knots of feeling are tied so tightly that they will never be loosened. The child begins to recognize a kinship with others, gradually becomes a moral being, and finds that he or she has a place in "the great mysterious incorporation of the human race". Through perseverance and effort, we pass on knowledge, values, attitudes, household gods. The child learns to learn and to concentrate, and acquires the habits and disciplines without which nothing is possible. We teach children to be competent persons. They learn the skills of knowing how to behave – the practical business of living which cannot be formulated in a phrase.

Without that start, children are forever handicapped, and statistically more prone to every kind of ill, from delinquency to unemployment, criminality, poor health and early death. Neglect of these early things, however, is increasing alarmingly. Nursery schools now report that children are arriving without being potty trained, and even unable to *speak*. Teachers now talk of children with "behavioural difficulties"; but behaving properly has not suddenly become difficult: the term is a euphemism for children who have not been disciplined and taught to behave. Parents are neglecting them, and in at least one respect public policy is virtually endorsing this neglect. Patricia Morgan has reported on findings from 88 studies, involving 22,000 children, which "concluded that regular non-parental care for more than 20 hours per week had an unmistakably detrimental effect on behaviour and attachment, and, to a lesser extent, on intellectual development" (*Prospect*, October 1996).

The early messages that many children receive from their parents are of isolation and separation. Many young people have grown up believing that to look after number one is the supreme virtue, and that to rely upon or devote oneself to others is the supreme folly. Children are given keys to let themselves in after school, when they are left unsupervised – provided for but not cared for. Many families have become shifting alliances which neglect the art of sharing. There is hardly time in today's calculated, crowded schedules. Parents and children are insulated from one another. As familial activities decline, there is less appreciation of the social value of taking the dog for a walk or playing cards. Even talking face to face is known to be in steep decline. With 24-hour services of all kinds available, there is no need for families to synchronize their days. People get up, go out, work, eat and go to sleep at times just to suit themselves, and the only rule is not to impinge upon anyone else. Electronic living – the Walkman, a television in every bedroom, the personal phone, the microwaveable video dinner – enables them to lock themselves away in a virtual life of perpetual solitude. They can occupy the same space without sharing it and the same days without ever coinciding. People are becoming alarmingly unsocial, even when they are together: a group of teenagers may consider it normal to travel together without conversing, each listening instead to music on a separate tape-recorder.

Even meals, which historically symbolize the fair sharing of the spoils and which have been important rituals in almost every culture, are rarely taken together by whole families. Roger Scruton has attacked this solipsism:

> This means that the most important moment of social renewal – on which families depend for their inner self-confidence, and on which serious friendships are built – is of increasingly marginal

> significance. Eating is becoming functional. . . It has become permissible to refuse what does not conform to our dietary principles. Vegetarians in general, and vegans in particular, have succeeded in moralizing the practice of eating in an individualistic direction. It has lost its character as a social ceremony in which our individualities are dissolved, and become an occasion for the public display of private fads.
>
> (*The Times*, June 17, 1996.)

If each member is apparently self-reliant, the family need have no consensus about anything, whether it be what to eat, which television programmes to watch or how to behave. But the result of this absence of mutual dependence is broken families, broken lives and a society broken down into its bewildered and lost individuals.

A boy is born illegitimate, the result of a casual encounter between a man who disappears and a mother who has divorced the father of her first two children and who subsequently marries a third man, who himself has other offspring. How can that boy know who he is? What is his place in the world, his home? And if he feels an outsider, what revenge might he one day exact? If Hobbes was right and man in a state of nature is ignorant, isolated and hostile, we are returning many in future generations to that state; if Burke was right and man is by nature social, we are denaturing ourselves.

William Godwin declared in his *Political Justice* that marriage and parental duties were irrational, and that one day men and women would act not so narrowly, but for the benefit of all. But science now has a rational explanation for parental altruism, based on the "coefficient of relatedness": parents are looking after the future of their genes. We have a stake not only in our personal welfare, but in that of others who share our make-up. So it really is our instinct and interest to nurture our own as well as ourselves. Biologically (though not in every case), parents have a deeper commitment than, say, step-parents. Our loyalties lie first with our blood-relatives, then with our extended families, and then with those who share our values – what we wish to replicate and perpetuate. This may be considered a reductionist and incomplete account (the love for adopted children, for instance, can be equally strong, though it is a deliberate choice); nevertheless, Godwin was wrong to suppose that we are tied to all others equally. To be evenhandedly concerned for every other human being is to deny one of our primary impulses.

Today, however, people are expected to extend an abstract charity and feel a universal benevolence. Loving our neighbours as ourselves is not so tall an order as what we are now told we must do, which is love those with whom we have nothing in common, who may impinge upon or rival or threaten us and our immediate circle, and of whom we are therefore suspicious. We are told we should be equally comfortable with all people, however alien their ways, and should not discriminate between people on any grounds – in which case we will never be close to anyone.

In his "Fragment of an *Antigone*", Matthew Arnold put the Burkean case against this rootlessness:

> For every day man may be link'd and loosed
> With strangers; but the bond
> Original, deep-inwound,
> Of blood, can he not bind,
> Nor, if Fate binds, not bear.

Our lives neither begin nor end with our lives. We cannot entirely escape what Arnold calls our "little companies" (recalling Burke's famous "little platoon") or "our own place". Yet today, partly due to abuse, many young people regard their own families with contempt, and cut themselves off from homes which they believe have limited their scope and growth. (Local authorities have been known to assist this severance by paying for them to change their names.) Many young people suppose, like Rousseau, that man is born free and yet finds himself in chains. They believe that as individuals they are the equal of anyone, and wish to be part simply of "youth culture" or the universal family. They want to make themselves, that is, into abstractions.

Burke himself opposed the oppression of a distant people as ardently as anyone before or since, and was of practical service to them. Yet he sarcastically attributed to Rousseau the "new-invented virtue" of "benevolence to the whole species, and want of feeling for every individual with whom the professors come in contact". This, he said, led Rousseau "constantly to exhaust the stores of his powerful rhetoric in the expression of universal benevolence, whilst his heart was incapable of harbouring one spark of common parental affection" – and this vitiation of the natural order has become increasingly common. Even Seamus Heaney, a poet who mulls continually over his childhood sense of place and belonging, can write, high-mindedly, "Who is my neighbour? My neighbour is all mankind." But this is impossibly Nobel. The Irish need to find ways to live with their neighbours; all mankind can come later. In caring supposedly for everyone, we forget how to care for particular people. What we need to hear preached is "Who is all mankind? All mankind starts with my neighbour."

Family feeling is inevitably weakened if sex is stripped of its commitments and reduced to an animal urge. Like Rousseau, fathers leave their families, with little guilt, to chase the rainbow of personal fulfilment. Men and women believe they have a "right" to "choose" – and then to change their minds: decisions and revisions which a minute will reverse. Having discarded traditional roles, they have no bank of experience to draw upon. Their moral choices, therefore, are supposed entirely subjective, like selecting fast-food or a car. Decisions profoundly affecting others rest upon private calculations and consciences, as the French revolutionaries argued that individuals should derive their moral principles solely from natural sentiment (i.e., present wishes) and reason. Burke saw that this philosophical relativism would have fearful practical consequences. He wrote in a letter of June 1, 1791:

> I have observed that the philosophers, in order to insinuate their polluted atheism into young minds, systematically flatter all their passions natural and unnatural. They explode or render odious or contemptible that class of virtues which restrain the appetite. These are at least nine out of ten of the virtues. In place of all these they substitute a virtue which they call humanity or benevolence. By these means, their morality has no idea in it of restraint, or indeed of a distinct settled principle of any kind. When their disciples are thus left free and guided only by present feeling, they are no longer to be depended on for good or evil.

He might have been describing the worst aspects of modern education, in which ingratiating teachers flatter their charges instead of instructing them. The fragile solitary ego is not to be imposed upon, but is left to manage as best it can, and as Burke expected, this is not very well. The self-educated are notoriously ignorant, and this applies also to moral self-education. This is what Burke called "*the philosophy of vanity*". People are no longer prepared to surrender to the common good their much treasured "natural right" as individuals to make their own mistakes about everything. Frustration is not to be countenanced, although it is a hallmark of civilization. At least nine out of ten of the virtues, Burke writes, are about restraint, but these have been made odious. Yet discipline – self-restraint – is what distinguishes liberty from licence. It is what makes freedom possible.

The relentless modern pressure to be "individual" leads to increasingly desperate and destructive attempts to stand out, and to pitifully predictable attempts to be different. Yet the signs are all on the outside. Imagined rejection of the orthodox shows itself not in thinking for oneself, but in dyed hair, bad clothes and bodily mutilation. This is a rejection, rather, of what the body urges for its own well-being, so it is not surprising that this cult of protest is so frequently self-destructive.

The young, of course, overestimate their originality. They haven't experience enough to realize that they are following in large footsteps. Teenagers imagine that they have invented sex, whereas a little reflection suggests it has been going on for a considerable time. There is an enormous waste involved in every generation having so laboriously to relearn these lessons (and, with them, a little humility). Studying history can be tedious when we are young, but it becomes more absorbing – like gardening – as we age.

> As we grow older
> The world becomes stranger, the pattern more complicated
> Of dead and living.
>
> (*East Coker.*)

Perhaps it is a pity that the experience of our ancestors cannot be passed on genetically, but for the moment even the scientists cannot change that fact. This does suggest, though, that we should not orientate society ever more towards the young. What do they know?

How we bring children into the world, and subsequently take responsibility for them is a critical test of our civilization and our belief in the future. The love of babies and children for their own sake brings no immediate return, but it is instinctive and spontaneous, and indicates our capacity for altruism, charity and social living. But over and over, one hears news of children injured or killed maliciously, or involved in some inexplicable cruelty, or of children out of control and terrorizing adults, or of the growth of child prostitution. And over and over again it emerges that the perpetrators or the victims, or both, are from broken or reconstructed homes, or are illegitimate, or were living with others in a "family" despite being unrelated. Our increasing awareness of such cases is unlikely to be entirely due to more comprehensive reporting. More probably, it has to do with the spread of domestic arrangements that we liberally pretend are normal but which lend themselves to catastrophe. Not everything that is common is normal. Evidence from the former director of the Health Advisory Service and from the British Psychological Society suggests – doubtless with some exaggeration – that "one child in four suffers mental disorders" (*The Sunday Telegraph*, December 1, 1996). Nothing like that many children are born with mental problems, so in many cases we are to blame for disturbing them.

Our society is obsessed with "child abuse". But the horror at certain narrow forms of this seems to be a virtually deliberate guilty evasion of the much more widespread assault on children's welfare: the untroubled acceptance of divorce, single parents, promiscuous fecundity, the economic pressure on mothers to go out to work. Divorce and illegitimacy exceed 50 per cent in some places, and mothers who are working or on benefit are in a majority. But what is prevalent is not necessarily good. It is quite possible, perhaps common, for whole generations and whole cultures to go astray. Reading Burke can persuade one that our culture took a critical wrong turning two centuries ago – which makes the aberration of fundamentalist feminism seem very brief.

In the *Reflections*, Burke emphasized the dependency of the state upon healthy domestic relations: "We have given to our frame of polity the image of a relation in blood; binding up the constitution of our country with our dearest domestic ties; adopting our fundamental laws into the bosom of our family affections". The dependency remains, and if the assertion of individual rights is liable to rend the fabric of our polity, the tears begin in families. If we cannot live within this most basic institution, then the larger institutions of state will never be secure. Whatever our atomized world pretends, the family, the social union and the continuance of tradition matter more than the individual. For without those, individuals and whole generations are crippled. Overcoming selfishness is a social achievement, but also a part of our better nature.

18

Where Now?

Whether Britain's present political system, or any future democracy, is more representative of all the interests of the nation or enjoys greater public confidence than the "mixed and tempered government" which Burke tried to uphold and which Coleridge lamented is an open question. Contempt for MPs is at least as great as ever.

It is still possible to see the middle period of the mixed constitution – 1689–1832 – as a time of stability when Britain achieved pre-eminence and prosperity. In a letter to Lord Sheffield on the first day of 1793, Gibbon paid tribute to this from abroad: "even as a citizen of the world, I wish the stability of England, the sole great refuge of mankind against the opposite mischiefs of despotism and democracy." But now the long historical transition from a belief in absolute monarchy to a belief in absolute democracy is almost complete. "These old fanatics of single arbitrary power dogmatized as if hereditary royalty was the only lawful government in the world," wrote Burke in the *Reflections*, "just as our new fanatics of popular arbitrary power maintain that a popular election is the sole lawful source of authority." The prerogatives which democracy asserts are the mirror image of the claims of feudal monarchs; the divine right of kings is being replaced by the *carte blanche* of prime ministers and bureaucrats. For as Burke saw, fundamentalist democracy is a kind of extremism. He shows why it must be restrained by the laws and constitution.

It takes no wisdom at all to wish for equality and liberty: the naïvest Jack Cade makes these his calls to arms. But to understand how a moderated liberty and equity can be sustained requires insight and experience. Because Burke's argument is more sophisticated than the "ignorant flippancy of Thomas Paine", he has always been less popular than his antagonist. What he stood for is very surprising – quite different from what most people suppose – and has largely been forgotten.

Misrepresentation of him as apologist for the *ancien régime* began early. In the debate on his *Speech on the Army Estimates* in February 1790, Burke turned upon his friend Sheridan, who had, he said,

> as cruelly as unexpectedly, misrepresented the nature of his remarks. The hon. gentleman had thought proper to charge him with being the advocate of despotism, though, in the beginning of his former speech, he had expressly reprobated every measure that carried with it even the slightest appearance of despotism. All who knew him could not avoid, without the most unnatural violation of natural justice, but acknowledge that he was the professed enemy of despotism, in every shape, whether, as he had before observed, it appeared as the splendid tyranny of Louis XIV, or the outrageous democracy of the present government of France, which levelled all distinctions in society.
>
> (*Parliamentary History*, XXVIII, 370.)

But the misrepresentation continued, inflaming Burke still further. And as he became more impassioned, lesser men began to speak of him as mad. Samuel Rogers' *Table-Talk* records the impression of a contemporary: "'Burke', observed Grattan, 'became at last such an enthusiastic admirer of kingly power, that he could not have slept comfortably on his pillow, if he had not thought that the King had a right to carry it off from under his head.'" It was not, however, subjects' pillows that were being carried off, but kings' heads, and Grattan's remark is animated by the excitement of the guillotine. From 1789 to the end of his life, Burke probably never did sleep comfortably, because of his sense that a delicate balance was jeopardized. The complacency is Grattan's.

One has only to read Burke to find that in rejecting the "new abuses", he was no "partisan of the old". He was the advocate of a third way. "Have these gentlemen", he asks, "never heard, in the whole circle of the world of theory and practice, of any thing between the despotism of the monarch and the despotism of the multitude?" He believed that the British possessed "an invaluable treasure" in a constitution that was fitted to their native character and situation, as well as to natural justice and the nature of man and society. As long as its balance was maintained, no arbitrary power could compromise British freedoms.

That balance is a moral question, too. People who overemphasize things that can be counted (money, votes) or written down (rights, entitlements) are liable to underestimate or even scorn values that are unquantifiable (experience, wisdom) or magnanimous (loyalty, clemency). As Burke remarked of "the tribe of vulgar politicians", in his *Letters on a Regicide Peace*, "They think there is nothing worth pursuit, but that which they can handle; which they can measure with a two-foot rule; which they can tell upon ten fingers." But if there is nothing more – if all that Burke comprehends as chivalry fails – then both private and public trust become almost impossible. People trained in cynicism become reluctant to entrust their interests, whether their deepest feelings of love or their political welfare, to others. So strains in the relations between the sexes or in families both parallel and contribute to social and political strains. The more people breach the many voluntary codes of honour and duty, the less we are able to rely on these codes. As more and more people act untrustworthily, trust becomes less and less rational. But just as rules can never take the place of conscience and self-restraint, a culture of formal rights and entitlements can never achieve the happiness of a culture in which respect is usually reciprocated by honour.

On one issue which troubled him, Burke was empirically wrong. Although he urged the abolition of slavery, he writes in the *Reflections* of the worst kinds of wage-slavery as immitigable, when he refers to those who work

> from dawn to dark in the innumerable servile, degrading, unseemly, unmanly, and often most unwholesome and pestiferous occupations to which by the social economy so many wretches are inevitably doomed. If it were not generally pernicious to disturb the natural course of things, and to impede, in any degree, the great wheel of circulation which is turned by the strangely directed labour of these unhappy people, I should be . . . inclined forcibly to rescue them from their miserable industry. . . It is a subject on which I have often reflected, and never reflected without feeling from it. I am sure that no consideration except the necessity of submitting to the yoke of luxury and the despotism of fancy, who in their own imperious way will distribute the surplus product of the soil, can justify the toleration of such trades and employments in a well-regulated state.

Burke's recoil of feeling does him credit, but he too easily concludes that the dark satanic mills are inevitable, and that Adam Smith's free market is a law of "the natural course of things" which can never be ameliorated by a second nature of legal institutions. For reforms in the 19th century showed that such degradations could be successfully outlawed. After writing in this too pessimistic, too dogmatic vein, Burke would be pleased to be proved wrong. Real progress in making people less wretched has been achieved. Yet the Factory Acts were specifics; they were not based on indefinitely extendable "rights". Technical advances have led to automation of many of the most miserable tasks. The shift from physical to intellectual work has extended opportunities for learning, creativity and a full life to far more people; and yet public standards of taste and judgment are being sacrificed as the media scramble to find the lowest, commonest denominator and the largest profit.

Throughout his life, Matthew Arnold was influenced by Burke, but in his social criticism he argued that "*the modern spirit*" was an irresistible force. The democracy that Burke had tried to forestall was pressing inexorably onwards throughout Europe – with France still in the vanguard, as a legacy of the revolution – and Arnold was not dismayed. Equality in France, he wrote in 1861,

> . . . has undoubtedly given to the lower classes, to the body of the common people, a self-respect, an enlargement of spirit, a consciousness of counting for something in their country's action, which has raised them in the scale of humanity. The common people, in France, seems to me the soundest part of the French nation. They seem to me more free from the two opposite degradations of multitudes, brutality and servility, to have a more developed human life, more of what distinguishes elsewhere the cultured classes from the vulgar, than the common people in any other country with which I am acquainted.
>
> ("Democracy".)

This optimistic picture of democracy, however, is not recognizable in Britain today. The present state of the common people would depress Arnold. For despite enormous efforts to help them to enjoy the benefits of a more developed life, through education and subsidized culture, there is a new and frightening brutalism. Increasingly the cultured classes are obliged to isolate themselves from a threatening barbarism. The middle classes are certainly larger than ever before, but there is little sign of Arnold's "enlargement of spirit" at the bottom of society. Instead there is a subculture of the worst possible vulgarity. The imagination of many people is bounded by money, gambling, fame, violence, sex, drink, television, true-life crime and sport. These titillations are the comprehensive recipe for a tabloid newspaper and a tabloid society.

This vast sub-culture is serviced by a terrible pact. Much of the worst material – whether it be junk television, lotteries, or the kind of "gangsta" music or pornography or computer-games that incite violence – is provided by a plutocracy which therefore has an apparent interest in its continuance. This new plutocracy is defined not so much by ownership of the means of production as by ownership of states of mind. With a short-sightedness comparable to that of the British fortune-hunters in Warren Hastings' India, a cultural plundering and despoiling is in progress. Wealthy companies are competing to lower standards and degrade tastes for profit. This is enrichment by impoverishment. The multitude do indeed count for something as never before; not, however, as conscientious individuals, but corporately as the providers of large fortunes and popular mandates. So the weight of the few exploiters and that of the many ready customers are exerted together. Business and money argue that what they provide is democratic and in demand; yet business interests are able to manipulate popular opinion. The age of sophisters, economists, and calculators has succeeded, as Burke so promptly predicted.

The question, then, must be how to counterbalance these degrading forces. Arnold tried out an answer:

> On what action may we rely to replace, for some time at any rate, that action of the aristocracy upon the people of this country, which we have seen exercise an influence in many respects elevating and beneficial, but which is rapidly, and from inevitable causes, ceasing? . . . I confess I am disposed to answer: On the action of the state.

Again, this optimism now looks misplaced. The experiment has been tried and is at best only partially successful. In this century we have seen how the power of the state, when misused, can be the most hideous of evils. But even the most benevolent state has great difficulty in "elevating" the brutish. Beveridge's welfare state aimed to vanquish the five giants of Want, Squalor, Ignorance, Disease and Idleness. Of these, Want and Disease were mitigated by public expenditure, but the more moral problems of Squalor, Ignorance and Idleness, people must conquer for themselves. Bitter experience shows that dependency expands to demand slightly more than the money available. And financial support can be a disincentive, robbing people of motivation and of their true freedom. For poverty, as Doug Bandow has written, involves much more than material want. There is also what he calls "behavioural poverty", which consists of "bad decisions, like having a child out of wedlock, committing crimes, failing to finish school, not working, and using drugs", and which may well be made worse by state financial provision. (*Freedom Today*, October 1996.)

Burke certainly believed that a state-contrived virtue was impossible, and he opposed managerialism. "It is better to cherish virtue and humanity by leaving much to free will, even with some loss to the object, than to attempt to make men mere machines and instruments of a political benevolence," the *Reflections* tell us. "The world on the whole will gain by a liberty without which virtue cannot exist."

Arnold thought the action of the state in France in 1861 was too powerful, but added, "I am very sure that, strengthen in England the action of the state as one may, it will always find itself sufficiently controlled." Now, however, the actions and managerial ambitions of the state and the superstate exceed anything he could have imagined. Government in Britain controls approximately 43 per cent of the economy; elsewhere in Europe the figure is higher yet. And while there have been successes in raising cultural and educational standards – notably the old BBC – scarcely anyone still believes in a paternalistic, benevolent state as the guardian of values, morality and wisdom. Nor does the state generally have conviction enough to stand up to the alliance of the underclass and the plunderclass.

The state must exercise controls, but there must also be controls upon it. How? The requirement for what Coleridge called "the triple assent" necessarily made legislating more difficult, and this was inherently advantageous. Without those other obstacles it is too easy for a ruling political party to whip ill-considered laws through the Commons. Today's MPs believe that they sit in the

House in order to legislate, rather than to debate, and accordingly we have far too many laws. Experience shows that laws passed in haste, or without proper debate or wide consent, tend shortly to be found ineffective or oppressive; they then have to be repealed at public expense, and to the detriment of parliamentary authority.

If policies still needed the endorsement of three competing interests, they would be continually monitored from three perspectives, and any not agreed to be of general national benefit could – given these safeguards – be modified by the flux of alliances. Such "conflicting interests", reflecting opposed forces outside Parliament, would in Burke's words, "render deliberation a matter not of choice, but of necessity".

Plates 14 and 15 of Nicholas K. Robinson's *Edmund Burke: A Life in Caricature* show the constitution conventionally represented as a tripod in cartoons of the 1770s, for a structure with three bases is inherently more stable than a monolith. Burke also uses a still better metaphor, taken from Ecclesiastes 4.12, when he refers to the three strands being woven into a much stronger "triple cord, which no man can break" (*Letter to a Noble Lord*). The nation, past, present and future, is a single cord, of which every fibre is a part: our interests can be successfully woven together. No faction or class is entire of itself, but every one is part of the whole, because we are involved with one another.

Burke's emphasis on a heterogeneous politics might usefully be translated into present circumstances. We cannot take directly from his age solutions to our very different problems – following Montesquieu, he emphasized that the politics of every age has its own character – but if some of his forms need to be discarded, we have yet much to gain from his principles. The triangulation offered by monarch, Lords and Commons may no longer be appropriate (or capable of rescue), but other principles of interest and authority might yet be permitted alongside that of democracy.

The British constitution has been immeasurably weakened by 25 years of European misadventures. Worse even than the overruling of legislative and judicial powers has been the loss of confidence in Parliament. The self-sufficiency of the nation has bled away. The process of sapping confidence by an astonishing presumption is the very one tried 200 years ago. To begin with, as Burke wrote in 1796, the usurpers "more directly undertake to be the real representatives of the people of this kingdom: and on a supposition in which they agree with our parliamentary reformers, that the House of Commons is not that representative, the function being vacant, they, as our true constitutional organ, inform His Majesty and the world of the sense of the nation." Just so today: Parliament is subverted from without and within, and the gullible look abroad for salvation. Once Parliament ceases to be the agreed focus of "the sense of the nation", because its powers have been exported, the plausibility of all kinds of systematic reforms is dangerously increased.

Furthermore, Parliament has abdicated many of its powers while retaining its privileges. Its appetite for legislation remains voracious, but it has condemned itself to ever-increasing interference in the trivial, and the effect is to magnify the stupidities of Europe.

But even leaving aside the disaster of the European Union, Britain's political arrangements are not working well. Burke's writings help to explain why. Two centuries of attachment to the simplicities of Paine have had the effect of weakening and further weakening the non-democratic elements of the state, so that now the Left can truly say that the constitution needs strengthening. It is true: reform is needed, but any conservative, or Burkean, must hesitate to say so, because all the schemes of reform that are on offer would make matters worse. The nation does not need to abolish the monarchy, or the voting rights of hereditary peers (with no idea of how to replace their restraining influence), or to introduce proportional representation or regional parliaments or "citizen's juries". It needs not an extension of democracy, but new counterbalances to democracy. It should have not fewer anomalies, but more – for many anomalies are correctives in disguise. Rather than our constitution being judged (and found wanting) by the purist criterion of democracy, democracy should be judged by criteria of consent and contentment. As Burke would have clearly seen, most current proposals for change are attempts to correct a system too reliant on a fickle and biddable popular opinion by relying upon it still further. Instead of refining our democracy, he would have us pause to ask, is democracy enough?

However, Burke never wrote about how we might *escape* what have become our present discontents. He wrote to save us from falling prey to them. He does not offer ready solutions to modern problems, although he does help to explain the errors in so many basic modern beliefs. If those errors and those beliefs can be extirpated, then perhaps contemporary solutions will start to emerge.

Rather than a method or calculus or ideology, Burke's message is a subtle one, responsive to circumstances. In a letter of July 22, 1791, he wrote: "But surely you forget, that I was throwing out reflections upon a political event, and not reading a lecture upon theorism and principles of government. How I should treat such a subject is not for me to say, for I never had that intention." Modern critics such as Michael Freeman or Padraig O'Brien may gratify themselves by juxtaposing passages so that Burke seems to contradict himself, but Burke did not seek a narrow consistency. He was alert to changing situations, and at different times he emphasized different principles, reflecting the complexity of human affairs. His ideas offer a restrained liberty and practical ways to reconcile stability with flexibility. The higher abstractions, which have preoccupied other political philosophers, he considered a snare. In the margin of an undated letter to Lord John Cavendish, Rockingham's Chancellor of the Exchequer, he wrote: "You know my opinions upon insulated morality and politics."

"Extremely often, in dealing with the world, one arrives at two ideas or ways of dealing with things which both work and are needed, but which entirely contradict one another," wrote the literary critic William Empson. "Very often in the past a new idea or way of dealing with things has been found, which includes the two old ones, and when you think back to them as particular cases they 'obviously' don't contradict any more" (*Granta*, March 9, 1928). Different ways of dealing with things may well need one another. Our courts, for instance, combine the legal knowledge of unelected judges (appointees from a specialist profession) with the native savvy of a random jury. As long as there are calls for change both from those, on the one hand, who believe that the legal profession needs to be "opened up" by positive discrimination to make it less élitist, and from those, on the other, who believe that the jury should be abolished in the most involved cases, because only the experts can understand them, the balance of principles is probably about right. But in political life, who now will follow Edmund Burke and say that the will of the mass must be counterbalanced?

Perhaps it will one day be possible again to venture that democracy need not be a contradiction of every other form of representation, and that it too might profitably be combined, as in the past it was, with complementary principles, which, in Burke's words, "may be various without being contrary to, or exclusive of each other". Despotism is not the sole alternative to absolute democracy, and a "despotic democracy" is not to be preferred to "a government of reciprocal control". It would be a triumph of freedom to establish once again a pluralist society of the kind that Edmund Burke argued for, so that every man might live under his fig or his vine tree in peace, and enjoy the fruits of his labour.

Select Bibliography

ARNOLD, MATTHEW, *Poetry and Prose*, ed. John Bryson, Reynard Library. London, 1954

AYLING, STANLEY, *Edmund Burke: His Life and Opinions*. London, 1988

BAGEHOT, WALTER, *The English Constitution*, with an introduction by Richard Crossman. London, 1963 (repr. 1993)

BERLIN, ISAIAH, "Nationalism" in *Against the Current: Essays in the History of Ideas*. London, 1979

BOOKER, CHRISTOPHER, and NORTH, RICHARD, *The Castle of Lies: Why Britain must get out of Europe*. London, 1996

BOSWELL, JAMES, *Life of Johnson*, ed. George Birkbeck Hill and L. F. Powell. 6 vols, Oxford, 1934–50

BRADFORD, WILLIAM, "Of Plimouth Plantation", in *The Faber Book of America*, ed. Christopher Ricks. London, 1992

BURKE, EDMUND, *The Correspondence of Edmund Burke*, gen. ed. Thomas W. Copeland. 10 vols, Cambridge, 1958–78

— *Selected Letters of Edmund Burke*, ed. Harvey C. Mansfield Jr. Chicago, 1984 (a selection from the *Correspondence*)

— *The Works of the Right Honourable Edmund Burke*, Bohn's British Classics. 8 vols, London, 1854–89

— *The Writings and Speeches of Edmund Burke*, gen. ed. Paul Langford. Oxford, 1981–

— *Reflections on the Revolution in France*, ed. Conor Cruise O'Brien. London, 1968

— *Further Reflections on the Revolution in France*, ed. Daniel E. Ritchie. Indianapolis, 1992

CAMPBELL, THOMAS, *Dr Campbell's Diary of a Visit to England in 1775*, ed. James L. Clifford. Cambridge, 1947

CHESTERTON, G. K., *Orthodoxy*. London, 1908

COLERIDGE, S. T., *Biographia Literaria*, ed. J. Shawcross. Oxford, 1907

— *Selected Letters*, ed. H. J. Jackson. Oxford, 1987

— *Specimens of the Table Talk of the Late Samuel Taylor Coleridge*. 2 vols, London, 1835

COPELAND, THOMAS W., *Edmund Burke: Six Essays*. London, 1950

COURTNEY, C. P., *Montesquieu and Burke*. Oxford, 1963

DE BRUYN, FRANS, *The Literary Genres of Edmund Burke: The Political Uses of Literary Form*. Oxford, 1996

ELIOT, T. S., *Collected Poems 1909–1962*. London, 1963

— "Tradition and the Individual Talent" in *Selected Essays*. London, 1932 (3rd ed. 1951)

EMPSON, WILLIAM, *Empson in Granta*. Tunbridge Wells, 1993

ENRIGHT, D. J., *Interplay*. Oxford, 1995
FREEMAN, MICHAEL, *Edmund Burke and the Critique of Political Radicalism*. Oxford, 1980
HAZLITT, WILLIAM, "Eloquence of the British Senate", in *Selected Essays* ed. Geoffrey Keynes, Nonesuch Press. London, 1930
JOHNSON, SAMUEL, *A Dictionary of the English Language*. London, 1755 (repr. 1828)
KENYON, J. P. (ed.), *The Stuart Constitution 1603–1688: Documents and Commentary*. Cambridge, 1966
LARKIN, PHILIP, *Collected Poems*. London, 1988
LEWIS, C. S., *The Four Loves*. London, 1960
LUCAS, PAUL, "On Edmund Burke's Doctrine of Prescription" in *The Historical Journal*, XI. Cambridge, 1968
MCKIBBEN, BILL, *The End of Nature*. London, 1990
MORLEY, JOHN, *Burke*, English Men of Letters series. London, 1888
— "Edmund Burke" in *The Dictionary of National Biography*. London, 1885–1900
NEWMAN, BERTRAM, *Edmund Burke*. London, 1927
O'BRIEN, CONOR CRUISE, *The Great Melody: A Thematic Biography of Edmund Burke*. London, 1992
O'BRIEN, P., *Debate Aborted, 1789–91: Priestley, Paine, Burke and the Revolution in France*. Durham, 1996
PAINE, THOMAS, *The Rights of Man*. London, 1791
Parliamentary History of England, 1066–1803. London, 1806–20 (forerunner of Hansard)
PARKIN, C. W., "Burke and the Conservative Tradition" in *Political Ideas*, ed. David Thomson. London, 1966 (repr. 1969)
PRIOR, JAMES, *Memoir of the Life and Character of the Right Hon. Edmund Burke*. London, 1824
PRYCE-JONES, DAVID, "Unrealism and Foreign Policy" in *Conservative Realism*, ed. Kenneth Minogue. London, 1996
REDFORD, BRUCE, *Venice & the Grand Tour*. Yale, 1996
RICKS, CHRISTOPHER *Essays in Appreciation*. Oxford, 1996
ROBINSON, NICHOLAS K., *Edmund Burke: A Life in Caricature*. New Haven, 1996
ROGERS, SAMUEL, *Recollections of the Table-Talk of Samuel Rogers*, ed. Alexander Dyce. London, 1856
STEPHEN, JAMES FITZJAMES, *Liberty, Fraternity, Equality*, ed. Stuart D. Warner. Indianapolis, 1993
TODD, WILLIAM B., *A Bibliography of Edmund Burke*. London, 1964 (2nd ed. 1982)

Index